New book releases are free the first 48 hours. Every month, there is a free download on Kindle. To know of new releases and dates for free downloads, please subscribe at

www.TessaCason.com

Tessa Cason
5694 Mission Ctr. Rd. #602-213
San Diego, CA. 92108
www.TessaCason.com
Tessa@TessaCason.com

© Tessa Cason, Little Sage Enterprises, LLC, 2022.

**All rights reserved.** No part of this work may be reproduced, published, or transmitted electronically without express written permission from the publisher.

Copyright of all images used in this book belong to their respective owners.

LEGAL NOTICE AND DISCLAIMER:

From author and publisher: The information in this book is not intended to diagnose or treat any particular disease and/or condition. Nothing contained herein is meant to replace qualified medical or psychological advice and/or services. The author and publisher do not assume responsibility for how the reader chooses to apply the techniques herein. Use of the information is at the reader's discretion and discernment. The author and publisher specifically disclaim any and all liability arising directly or indirectly from the use or application contained in this book.

Nothing contained in this book is to be considered medical advice for any specific situation. This information is not intended as a substitute for the advice or medical care of a Physician prior to taking any personal action with respect to the information contained in this book. This book and all of its contents are intended for educational and informational purpose only. The information in this book is believed to be reliable, but is presented without guaranty or warranty.

By reading further, you agree to release the author and publisher from any damages or injury associated with your use of the material in this book.

# 240 EFT Tapping Statements™ for Fear

Tessa Cason, MA

# My EFT Tapping Story

I established a life coaching practice in 1996 when life coaching was in its infancy. After several years, I realized that desire, exploration, and awareness did not equate to change and transformation for my clients.

Exploring the underlying cause of their pain, knowing their motivation to change, and defining who they wanted to become, did not create the changes in their lives they desired.

My livelihood was depended on the success of my clients. I realized I needed a tool or technique or method to aid my clients in their quest for change.

At the time, I knew that everything in our lives, all of our thoughts and feelings, choices and decisions, habits and experiences, actions and reactions were the result of our beliefs.

I knew that the beliefs were "stored" in our subconscious mind.

I knew that to transform and change our lives, we needed to heal the underlying unhealthy, dysfunctional beliefs on the subconscious level. I needed a tool, technique, or method to eliminate and heal the beliefs stored in the subconscious mind.

I visited a friend who managed a bookstore and told her of my dilemma, that I needed something to help my clients truly change and transform their lives. She reached for a book on the counter, near the register. "People have been raving about this book on EFT, Emotional Freedom Technique. Try it and see if it can help your clients."

In the 1990s, the internet was not an everyday part of our lives. Popular books sold more by word of mouth than any other means. Managing a bookstore, my friend knew what worked and what did not work. I trusted my friend, so I purchased the book.

As I read the book and discovered that EFT was tapping our head, I was unsure if this was the technique that would help my clients. I had some adventurous and forgiving clients whom I taught how to tap. When **every single client** returned for their next appointment and shared how different their lives had been that week because of tapping, I took notice! I was intrigued.

I learned that the first statement we needed to tap was: "It's not okay or safe for my life to change."

I learned that when a tapping statement did not clear, it meant there were other dysfunctional beliefs preventing the statement from clearing. When a statement didn't clear, I turned the statement into a question.

I learned that for EFT Tapping to work, we needed to find the cause of an issue.

I learned that clearing an emotional memory was different from clearing dysfunctional beliefs.

I learned that tapping one side of the body was more effective that tapping both sides simultaneously.

Clients started asking for tapping homework. I wrote out statements for them to tap. Soon, I had a library of tapping statements on different emotional issues.

I have been an EFT Practitioner since 2000. Working with hundreds of clients, one-on-one, I learned how to successfully utilize EFT so my clients could grow and transform their lives.

# Table of Contents

- 1    Chapter 1 – Intro
- 2    Chapter 2 – Lanie and Lennie's Story

- 14    Chapter 3 – EFT Tapping – Emotional Freedom Technique
- 15           How to Tap Short Form of EFT
- 17    Chapter 4 – EFT Tapping, Beliefs, and Subconscious Mind
- 19    Chapter 5 – How Does EFT Tapping Works?
- 20    Chapter 6 – Benefits of Using EFT Tapping
- 21    Chapter 7 – What We Say As We Tap Is Very Important
- 22    Chapter 8 – Using a Negative EFT Tapping Statement
- 23    Chapter 9 – Tapping Statements Are Most Effective When They Agree with Current Beliefs
- 24    Chapter 10 – The Very First EFT Tapping Statement to Tap
- 25    Chapter 11 – One Statement per Round of EFT vs Multiple Statements per Round of EFT
- 28    Chapter 12 – Walking Backwards EFT (Backing Up)
- 29    Chapter 13 – Intensity Level
- 30    Chapter 14 – Yawning While Tapping and Deep Breath After Tapping
- 31    Chapter 15 – Integration…What Happens After Tapping
- 32    Chapter 16 – EFT Tapping Doesn't Work for Me
- 33    Chapter 17 – What To Do if an EFT Tapping Statement Does Not Clear
- 34    Chapter 18 – Science and EFT Tapping Research
- 35    Chapter 19 – Is Lowering the Cortisol Level Enough to Permanently Change Our Lives?
- 36    Chapter 20 – Tapping Affirmations
- 37    Chapter 21 – Finishing Touches – Positive Statements

- 39    How to Use This Book

- 40    EFT Tapping Statements and Journaling Pages

- 64    Books by Tessa Cason

# Chapter 1
# Intro

Fear is an overwhelming feeling that can bring on a sense of dread, knots in the stomach, chills down the spine, or even the inability to breathe. We all know it. Fight-Flight-Freeze.

All fears begin as anxiety. Anxiety is the combination of unidentified anger, self-pity, hurt, and/or fear. Fear is something tangible, whereas anxiety is intangible; it is something that is difficult to put your finger on. Fear is anxiety that has found a specific threat to respond to.

Fear does not exist in the present. Fear puts us in the future. Something from the past has been remembered. This memory triggers the fear that the same thing will happen again.

We may be fearful that the ending this time won't be any different than it was before. We may be fearful we will have to go through the same situation again and won't be able to handle it any better than last time. We may be fearful that we will experience the same pain, hurt, and devastation all over again.

Fear is a self-protection mechanism. It is an internal alarm system that alerts us to potential harm. When we are in the present, we have the courage, discernment, awareness, wisdom, and confidence to identify and handle things that can cause us harm.

If we keep doing what we are doing, we will continue to get what we already have. If we don't want what we already have, we have to change the dysfunctional beliefs causing us harm on a subconscious level.

To make changes in our lives, we have to recognize, acknowledge, and take ownership of that which we want to transform. To make changes in our lives, we need a tool that will change the dysfunctional beliefs on a subconscious level.

EFT Tapping is one such tool that allows you to transform dysfunctional beliefs on a subconscious level. EFT tapping will help transform your fears and bring you into the present time where you have discernment, wisdom, and the confidence to deal with that which could harm you.

# Chapter 2
# Lanie and Lennie's

"So, it's true. The school district downsized the music department," Lanie sighs as she sees her husband's face.

"Not only the music department but the art department, English department, and the history department. Four of us in all. The latest hires. Last hired, first fired," says Lennie with a weak smile.

Lennie sits down on the couch next to his wife as she asks, "what now?"

He deeply exhales. "Well, there are two more months until school is out. Guess it's time to update my resume."

Putting on a brave face, Lanie turns to him and says, "we can work on your resume tomorrow before we take Gracie to the park. I can type it up."

"I am so sorry, Lanie," Lennie says as he looks down at their hands entwined together.

"Oh, no Lennie. It's not your fault. You didn't do anything wrong." Lanie reaches over and lifts her husband's face. "It's not your fault. You will find another job before the summer starts."

"I wish I had your enthusiasm. Music teachers are not in demand. I don't know how to do anything else, Lanie. Being a music teacher is the only thing I know."

"Lennie, we will make it work. I know we will," Lanie says encouragingly.

Lennie looks up, "we will start with updating my resume tomorrow. Then I will start applying for jobs."

Lanie adds, "if need be, I will get a job. I worked before we had Gracie after all."

"But I don't want you to get a job. You love being a stay-at-home mom with Gracie. She needs you here when she comes home from school. She's only in the first grade now."

In a serious tone, Lanie responds, "Lennie, if you are not able to find a job by the time school ends, let's consider me getting a job. I can work."

"But, who would take care of Gracie if you go back to work?" asks Lennie out of concern.

©Tessa Cason, 2021.

"Let's cross that bridge if we come to it. Dinner is about ready. Can you go get Gracie and help her wash her hands?"

Lanie moves off to the kitchen as Lennie walks to the bedroom to find Gracie.

*******************

"Lennie," Lanie starts, "it's been a month. You've posted your resume on all the websites, you've sent resumes off, we've dropped them off at all the music schools, senior centers, and even music stores without success." She sighs. "Maybe it's time I start looking for a job."

Joining Lanie in the kitchen to help prepare breakfast, Lennie turns to her. "Not yet. It's only been a month. Let's wait another week or so."

"Well, what about the idea of teaching private students?"

Lennie seems dispirited. "How would I find students? It seems overwhelming to start a business. We need a steady income. And there's no guarantee that anyone would want lessons from me. I don't have any place to teach them. I would have to teach the students in their home, which would be costly time-wise and financially to travel to students' homes. No. I don't think it's a good idea," Lennie turns back to flip the pancakes.

As Gracie comes into the kitchen for her breakfast, Lanie says, "Okay, we'll table the topic for now."

Lennie was privately worried. Nothing had come from applying for the few music teacher positions he had found online and in the paper. He really wasn't sure what to do. After all, he had a family to support.

Fear started to creep into his mind. What if he couldn't ever find a job in music again? He wasn't qualified to do anything different. They had a little bit of savings between them, but not enough to support them more than a couple of months. Get a job as a salesman? He didn't know how to sell. Get a job as a laborer? His hands were for playing instruments, not planting flowers.

Lennie could hear Lanie and Gracie at the kitchen table laughing as they ate the pancakes he made and talking about going to the park after breakfast.

Anxiety was taking over Lennie's thoughts. "I will never find a job and be able to support my family. I'm scared. What if I can't find a job?" As a chill runs through his whole body, Lennie has a sudden realization. "Oh my God, we could end up homeless if I can't find a job."

Flipping more pancakes, he didn't dare turn around and let his wife see the fear on his face. He was quietly panicking as the single word "homeless" looped in his mind over and over.

***********************

©Tessa Cason, 2021.

A month later, Lennie was at the graduation ceremony of his school. Lanie had dropped Gracie at a friend's house so that the children could have a play date. She wanted to have some alone time with Lennie when he returned.

When Lennie arrives home, he expects to see both Lanie and Gracie. Giving his wife a hug, he asks, "where is Gracie? In her room?"

After hugging her husband, and moving toward the couch, she says, "Join me on the couch. We need to talk."

A chill ran through his body again. Lennie hadn't heard those words in a long time. "We have to talk?" Moving to sit down next to her, he could feel the fear - a dagger that pierced his heart.

The reality was he had not been able to find a job. He had even started applying for jobs that he had never done before. He had not even received a nibble. No interviews. Not one person interested in his abilities, talents, or his needs. Fear. He could feel the fear as his stomach was in knots.

With compassion in her voice, she starts, "Lennie, I know you have been applying to lots of different jobs, and not just music jobs. I know there hasn't been much interest on the part of potential employers."

With tears welling up in his eyes, he looks down at his empty hands. He feels like he has failed his family. "She's going to tell me she's disappointed in me," he thinks to himself.

"Lennie, I love you so much. I love being married to you. I love being a family," says Lanie. "You have been putting a lot of pressure on yourself to find a job. I know you want to work."

As tears fall down his face, Lennie says, "I do want to work. I want to be able to support my family."

Wiping away the tears, Lanie says, "Lennie, you love music. You would not be happy doing anything else other than being a music teacher. It wouldn't be fair for you to take any job just to support our family."

"Lanie, it's my responsibility as a husband and father to support my family. I will take any job I can find at this point."

Putting her finger up to his lips, she says, "shhh. Please listen."

Lennie lifts his head to look at his beautiful, caring, compassionate wife. The last person in the world he wants to disappoint is Lanie. He loves her so much.

©Tessa Cason, 2021.

When she has her husband's attention, she makes eye contact and says, "I was offered my old job at the hotel. I accepted the position. I start on Monday."

Shock fills Lennie's eye. Wanting to protest, he opens his mouth to speak but Lanie interjects. "I have a plan."

With resignation, Lennie says, "A plan? You have a plan?"

Lanie begins, "The hotel will be flexible with my hours. I will work while Gracie is in school and on the weekends."

"The weekends?" asks Lennie. "You love the weekends when we take Gracie to the park."

"We have to do what needs to be done at this time. There's more to my plan."

Lennie exhales. He is awash with emotions. Sadness that he can't find a job. Fear that they could end up homeless. Hopelessness that their lives are heading downhill with nothing in sight to lift them up.

Lanie pauses before delivering what she knows will be the hardest part of the plan for Lennie to handle. Taking a deep breath, she continues, "I think we need to move to a smaller home. My housekeeping position will not cover all of our monthly expenses."

"Move?" He was taken aback. "But you love this house. Gracie has friends that live in the neighborhood. Where would we move to? It's expensive to move. First and last month's rent. Deposit. How can we afford it?" he says as his fear nears an all-time high.

"Wait. There's more to it," says Lanie.

"More? I'm not sure I can handle anymore," Lennie replies out of disbelief.

"Take a deep breath, Lennie," encourages Lanie. "Now exhale. Good."

She continues, "okay. Since I will be working, you can use that time to find us a place to live that is less expensive. You can also start packing. We have way too much stuff anyhow. There's stuff we can give away that we no longer need. We don't need to carry unneeded things to our new home."

With little enthusiasm, Lennie reluctantly accepts what he is hearing. "Okay, I will do my part. I will start looking for a new home and sorting through our stuff."

"There's one more thing," Lanie says as she walks towards their desk and retrieves a flyer. She hands it to Lennie and allows him to read it as she sits down next to him.

"What's this? A flyer for me to teach private lessons? Did you create this?" he asks in amazement.

Proudly, Lanie responds, "Yes, I did. You know how much I love doing graphics on the computer." She stays silent to allow Lennie a minute to process the news.

"Me? Teach private lessons? How am I going to find students?" Lennie continues to focus on the flyer, feeling totally inadequate. Once again, fear creeps into the pit of his stomach and a chill runs down his spine.

"How is this going to support us? I don't want you working to help support the family. I want to be able to find a job that will allow you to stay at home with Gracie."

This was not the reaction she was expecting. She heard the fear in his voice. Pure fear. "Now what?" she thought. How could she have been so wrong? She thought he would be thrilled that she was encouraging him to pursue what he loved to do - music and teaching.

Stunned, she takes a moment to find her words. "I thought this would have pleased you. I wanted you to know that I was all in favor of you starting your own business teaching music."

Too upset to talk, Lennie can only manage to say, "give me a minute." He then walks outside and takes a seat on the porch steps. He drops his head into his hands as he holds back tears. It was a lot to take in... his wife getting a job, and being forced to move to a smaller, more affordable home, all because he couldn't support his family. And now, she wants him to start his own business.

Lennie is paralyzed by fear. It feels as if the sky is falling and the walls are closing in. He tries to take a deep breath, but his rib cage freezes and wouldn't expand to let in any air.

Only once before had he been as scared as this. In high school, his parents were in a car accident. They survived, but he lived in fear until both his parents were healed and back home.

Emptiness and horrible feelings consume Lennie. He feels like he is falling down a rabbit hole never to be seen again.

As he hears Lanie's footsteps approach, he tries to pull it together. Lanie sits down next to Lennie and asks if he wants to talk.

Taking a deep breath, Lennie has a moment of complete honesty with her. He tells Lanie about his fears. That he's afraid he will never find another job, that they will end up homeless, and she will no longer love him because she is forced to go back to work because of his failures.

With gentleness, Lanie responds calmly, "I remember a saying when I was in college. It was this: 'The game of life doesn't build character. It reveals it.' The situation we find ourselves in is not of your making." She pauses. "Lennie, you didn't gamble your paycheck away. You didn't get yourself fired for incompetence. Life happens. The school district downsized. You were let go because, as you said, 'last hired, first fired.' You were not fired because you are incompetent."

"I understand what you are saying." Lennie replies. "I know the game of life reveals who we are. But I'm still afraid, Lanie. It feels like life is revealing that I am a coward and I'm having difficulty finding my courage. I'm paralyzed and unable to move forward." Lanie turns to him, "so what do you want to do now, Lennie?"

Without hesitating, Lennie answers, "I want everything to be as it was. I want a paycheck for doing what I love and have been trained to do. I want to be able to support my family without my wife having to go back to work. I want to continue to live in our home."

Softly, Lanie asks, "how likely will any of this happen in the very near future?"

"I know. I know. My head is buried in the sand," he says.

"Getting gritty yet? When do you think it might be a good idea to pull your head up out of the sand?" says a laughing Lanie.

Lennie laughs along with her. "Guess I have been in denial. I have been hoping that something would happen and I would be rehired. Well, that didn't happen. Guess I have to be realistic."

"Lennie, can I ask you a question?"

Leaning over, he gives his wife a kiss on the cheek he says, "Anything."

"I have to admit, I was really surprised by your reaction to the flyer that I created for you. I thought you would be pleased. I wanted to show you that I was supportive of you building a business teaching music."

Lennie takes her hand that was sitting on his thigh. "It takes a lot of energy to build a business. How can I focus on building a business and still look for a job with a steady paycheck? I wouldn't know how to build a business. I've always earned a paycheck. It's too risky for me to start a business."

"Okay, the excuses I hear are that you're used to earning a paycheck and it's too risky to start a business. Anything else?" asks Lanie.

Thinking about her question, Lennie adds, "I don't know how to start a business, Lanie. I don't know how to find students. A paycheck is more secure."

©Tessa Cason, 2021.

Smiling, Lanie says, "A paycheck is more secure. Someone else can make decisions, but regardless of your talent and abilities, you could be out of a job. You are now out of a job because someone made a decision to downsize the music department at your school."

Exhaling, Lennie agrees with her. He continues, "Lanie, I don't think I have the courage to be self-employed, to depend on myself to earn a substantial income to support my family."

With excitement, Lanie suddenly has a thought, "Hey! Let's invite Deborah and Hunter to lunch after church tomorrow. Hunter was downsized from his job a few years ago and is now self-employed. What do you think?"

"Okay. I'll call Hunter now to see if they are available for lunch tomorrow." Lennie pulls out his phone to call Hunter, and makes plan to meet with them after church tomorrow.

The next day at lunch with Hunter and Deborah, Lanie explains that Lennie had just been downsized from his job teaching music at the high school.

"Oh, Lennie, I'm so sorry. Any luck finding a new position?" asks Deborah.

Lennie responds, "None. I have applied for music and non-music teaching jobs without any success."

Turning to Hunter, Lanie says, "Hunter, when you were downsized from your job a few years ago and weren't able to find a job, you started your own business, didn't you?" Lanie pulls out the flyer that she made for Lennie and slides it in front of Hunter and Deborah.

Immediately, Deborah's eyes light up. "What a fabulous idea! Even in our church, there are parents that would hire you to teach music to their children in an instant."

Hunter nods his head in agreement.

Hesitant, Lennie says, "I don't know, Hunter. You have the courage to be self-employed. I am not comfortable depending on myself to create my own income. Truthfully, it scares me a lot. I've always had a job where someone handed me a paycheck."

At that point Deborah offers a suggestion. "Lennie, what if you put up a few flyers while still looking for a job? That way, not all your eggs are in one basket. Lanie did a fabulous job creating an enticing flyer."

Thinking about it, Lennie finally responds, "well, I think I can do that."

Deborah suggests putting a flyer on the church bulletin board after lunch, and Hunter offers to help with any business details.

Before retrieving Gracie from the daycare center at the church, Lennie and Lanie follow through on Deborah's suggestion of posting a flyer on the church bulletin board. The pastor is walking by when Lanie and Lennie are putting up the flyer. "Oh, Lennie, what a wonderful idea," says the pastor passing by. "No one knows this yet, but we lost our music director. Would you consider the position? Unfortunately, it's a non-paying position, but it could be an opportunity for networking."

With glee, Lanie says, "What a wonderful opportunity! Thank you for asking, pastor."

"Well, I guess you have a new music director," Lennie says, smiling widely.

The minister asks, "Can you get started now? Even though it is only June, there are a group of people meeting for the first time today to start planning the Christmas show. Lanie, do you have any interest in being a part of the planning meeting?"

Lanie hesitated before saying, "I do. How much longer is the day care center going to be open today?"

The minister smiled. "You're in luck. It will be open until the meeting ends."

"Then lead on, minister! You now have two new members on the committee," says Lanie.

The room is full of happy people chatting with each other as they wait for the minister to arrive. When he enters the room, everyone finds a seat ready for the meeting to begin.

"We are going to start the meeting by each of us introducing ourselves. Most of you know each other, but just in case there are some you don't know." With a happy grin on his face, he adds, "A few of you know that our Music Director just recently moved out of town and we were in need of a new Director. Notice the past tense. We 'were' in need of a new Director. Past tense because Lennie here has agreed to become our new Music Director. Lennie, why don't you start off the introductions?"

At the end of the meeting, everyone in the room congratulates Lennie on his new position before leaving the room. Paul waits to be the last to congratulate him and speak to Lennie. Paul and Lennie are acquaintances that see each other at church every Sunday. As Paul approaches, Lanie excuses herself so she can retrieve Gracie from the church's daycare center.

Paul begins, "congratulations on your new position in the church. With your music and teaching background, you will be a valuable asset for the church and the rest of us that have little musical experience and talent."

"Thank you," says Lennie graciously.

"You said in your introduction that you were beginning to take on students. I would like to be your first," says Paul.

"Really? Seriously? Wow." Lennie was taken aback. "I don't know what to say."

"Well, you can say 'yes' to begin with," laughs Paul.

"Truthfully," a hesitant Lennie begins, "I'm not sure how these sessions would work. Do I have to set up an official business? I don't have any place to teach… so I would have to use the students' homes."

Paul adds, "Well, you can certainly come to my home. I have a piano ready to go and I'm looking for piano lessons. Do you need payment upfront?"

"Oh. Money," says an overwhelmed Lennie. "You know, Paul, I'm not comfortable charging since this whole teaching lessons thing is such an unknown to me. How about I don't charge you for the lessons, if you allow me to explore how to do the whole teaching private lesson thing."

"Well," Paul ponders for a moment. "I understand your dilemma. But I feel you should receive something in return for your time and effort. What if we do an exchange?"

"An exchange? What do you mean?" says Lennie.

Paul replies, "well, I am an EFT Tapping Practitioner. EFT stands for Emotional Freedom Technique. It's a simple, yet highly effective technique that allows you to change dysfunctional beliefs and emotions on a subconscious level. We can work on any issues that you might want to work through."

"Oh, like therapy or counselling?" asks Lennie.

"Right, like therapy or counselling. I am a life coach."

"Wow. Well? Great timing," says Lennie. "I definitely think that if Lanie was here she would say 'yes'." He laughs. So my answer is, 'When can we get started?' I'm available."

"The sooner the better, in my case," says Paul.

Paul asks Lennie what his schedule is like. Lennie answers, "Well, when school ended, I became unemployed."

Paul and Lennie set up some time for the following Wednesday morning for their very first piano lessons and EFT Tapping sessions.

The following three months were like none other that Lennie had ever experienced. He did find a smaller, less expensive home. He did most of the sorting and packing. Every Sunday after service, Hunter, Deborah, Lanie, and Lennie had lunch and talked about setting up a business. Hunter insisted that Lennie set up a website once he was clear on what he wanted to offer.

©Tessa Cason, 2021.

Despite good progress on the business front, there was still no job interviews or possible positions anywhere in the music field for him, except at the church. The minister asked Lennie if he would teach music classes at the church. From teaching the classes, several of his students asked if he would teach them privately.

Most of all at this time, Lennie looked forward to Wednesday mornings. Since he had taken music classes as a child, he had a sense of how to structure a lesson. Paul was extremely helpful with feedback as to what would make a lesson more valuable for a student.

Wednesday mornings after the music lessons, Paul and Lennie switch hats. Paul becomes the Life Coach and Lennie becomes the student. Lennie really enjoyed the tapping. It was unlike anything he had experienced before. The day after a tapping session, he always felt stronger than before.

He dealt with his fears and practiced his tapping statements. Some of his favorites were:
* I am afraid of the unknown.
* I am paralyzed by fear.
* I don't trust that I can earn a living doing what I love.
* I'm afraid of being homeless.
* I hate that my wife has to work.
* The older I get, the more fearful I become.
* Starting my own business is scary.
* My fear is stopping me from moving forward.

Who knew exploring yourself would be so much fun. Well, probably lots of others. Coming from a family that "stoic" was their favorite way to be. He had never been exposed to anyone on the path of self-exploration.

With Hunter's and Paul's valuable insights and feedback, Lennie was slowly becoming more creative, more expressive, and more confident. But most importantly he was becoming less scared. He took it upon himself to learn about marketing, social media, and websites. Lanie, with her love for graphics, even offered to design a website for him.

Lennie wrote out lesson plans for Paul and left him material for homework. At that point Paul had enough lessons plans and homework material to fill a book! One day, Paul asks Lennie at the end of one of their sessions, "have you thought of ever publishing your lesson plans?"

"Publish my lesson plans?" Lennie is both shocked and amused. "Do you think there is a market for such a thing?" he asks.

"I don't know," responds Paul. "Lanie loves to explore the internet. Have her do some research to see what's available for people that want to learn music but who may not be able to afford a teacher. Have you ever thought of giving lessons via skype?"

©Tessa Cason, 2021.

"Skype? I've heard of it, but I'm not sure what it is," Lennie admits.

"Here is my username on Skype. When you get home today, call me via Skype. You can try it out."

"Hum, can you show me how to set up Skype on my computer?" asks Lennie. "Sure," Paul says, immediately flipping open his laptop.

On the way home, Lennie ponders the questions that Paul asked about publishing and teaching music via the internet. He discusses the idea with Lanie that night right after putting Gracie to bed. Lanie loves the idea.

"Ever since you started tapping with Paul, your fears are diminishing and your creativity has improved. Hunter, Deborah, and Paul have all suggested doing a business plan. Let's sit down and start writing one tonight!"

Lennie responds, "Another idea I had on the way home was to contact the English and Art teachers that also were downsized last summer. We've been emailing each other encouragement while looking for new jobs. Neither of them have found positions in their preferred subjects either."

Excitedly, Lanie responds, "What a fabulous idea. They can help you put together the material to be published."

"My thoughts, exactly," says a smiling Lennie. "Both of them are very talented. The art teacher also taught photography and I know he could add some valuable photos to the material. My creativity does not extend to writing, but I do know that the English teacher writes very well. He wrote some articles that were published in the school paper."

Before the night ended, Lanie and Lennie have developed a business plan from all the ideas and suggestions from Hunter, Deborah, and Paul. Lanie referred to the notes she took at each meeting they had with Hunter and Deborah. Lennie was able to recall most of Paul's suggestions. Their business plan was a roadmap for them that included marketing, social media, and how they would build the business.

The next day, Lennie sends off an email to both the Art and English teachers who respond quickly with great enthusiasm. The project was officially a "go!" Within a month, everything was completed in the form of music lesson books for adults and children, and were ready to be sold on Amazon. The project was so much fun the trio decided to create a series of books.

One of their marketing strategies was to contact moms who were homeschooling that needed a resource for music. One mom loved the material so much that she told other homeschool moms, leading this to become a consistent source of income for Lennie.

By the time the lease was up on the smaller home, Lennie was finally earning enough income from Amazon, private lessons, and their website to be able to move into a spacious house across the street from the park that Gracie loved so much.

> If a man harbors any sort of fear, it percolates through all his thinking, damages his personality, and makes him landlord to a ghost.
>
> Lloyd Cassel Douglas

# Chapter 3
# EFT Tapping – Emotional Freedom Technique

EFT Tapping is a very easy technique to learn. It involves making a statement as we contact the body by either circling or tapping.

An EFT Tapping Statement has three parts:

Part 1: starts with "**Even though**" followed by

Part 2: a statement which could be the **dysfunctional emotion or belief**, and

Part 3: ends with "**I totally and completely accept myself.**"

A complete statement would be, "**Even though I fear change, I totally and completely accept myself.**"

## Instruction for the Short Form of EFT Tapping

The instructions below are for using the right hand. Reverse the directions to tap using the left hand. It is more effective, when we tap, to tap only one side rather than both.

I. SET UP – BEGIN WITH CIRCLING OR TAPPING THE SIDE OF THE HAND:

  A. With the fingertips of the right hand, find a tender spot below the left collar bone. Once the tender spot is identified, press firmly on the spot, moving the fingertips in a circular motion toward the left shoulder, toward the outside, clockwise. Tapping the side of the hand can also be used instead of the circling.

  B. As the fingers circle and press against the tender spot or tap the side of the hand, repeat the tapping statement three times: "Even though,____[tapping statement]____, I totally and completely accept myself." An example would be: "Even though I fear change, I totally and completely accept myself."

Side of the hand

Tender spot below the left collar bone

©Tessa Cason, 2022.

II. TAPPING:
   A. After the third time, tap the following eight points, repeating the [tapping statement] at each point. Tap each point five – ten times:
      1. The inner edge of the eyebrow, just above the eye. [I fear change.]
      2. Temple, just to the side of the eye. [I fear change.]
      3. Just below the eye (on the cheekbone). [I fear change.]
      4. Under the nose. [I fear change.]
      5. Under the lips. [I fear change.]
      6. Under the knob of the collar bone. [I fear change.]
      7. Three inches under the arm pit. [I fear change.]
      8. Top back of the head. [I fear change.]

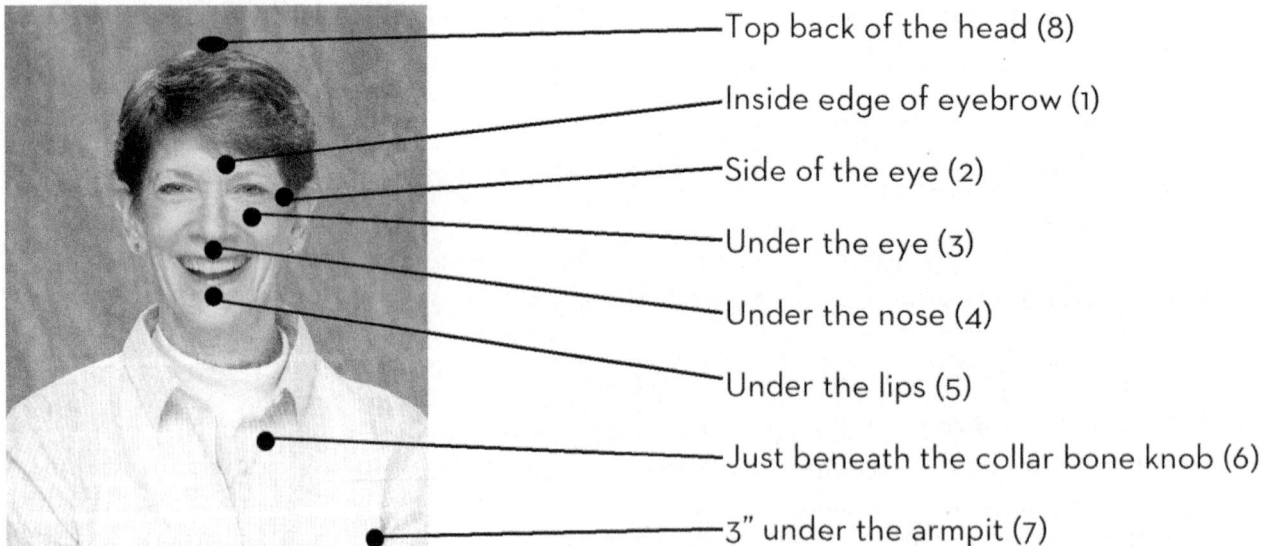

   B. After tapping, take a deep breath. If you are not able to take a deep, full, satisfying breath, do eye rolls.

III. EYE ROLLS
   A. With one hand tap continuously on the **back** of the other hand between the fourth and fifth fingers.
   B. Hold your head straight forward, eyes looking straight down.
   C. For six seconds, roll your eyes from the floor straight up toward the ceiling while repeating the tapping statement. Keep the head straight forward, only moving the eyes.

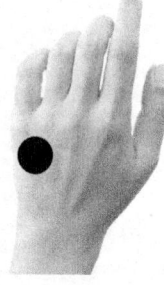

IV. TAKE ANOTHER DEEP BREATH.

©Tessa Cason, 2022.

# Chapter 4
# EFT Tapping, Beliefs, and the Subconscious Mind

## EFT – Emotional Freedom Technique

EFT is a technique that allows us to change dysfunctional beliefs and emotions on a subconscious level. It involves making a statement while tapping different points along meridian paths.

The general principle behind EFT is that the cause of all negative emotions is a disruption in the body's energy system. By tapping on locations where several different meridians flow, we can release unproductive memories, emotions, and beliefs that cause the blockages.

## A Belief is...

**A belief** is a mental acceptance of, and conviction in, the Truth, actuality, or validity of something. It is what we believe to be true, whether it is Truth or not. A belief is a thought that influences energy all the time.

## A Dysfunctional Belief is...

**A dysfunctional belief** is a belief that takes us away from peace, love, joy, stability, acceptance, and harmony. It causes us to feel stressed, fearful, anxious, and/or insecure.

## The Conscious Mind is...

The conscious mind is the part of us that thinks, passes judgments, makes decisions, remembers, analyzes, has desires, and communicates with others. It is responsible for logic and reasoning, understanding and comprehension. The mind determines our actions, feelings, thoughts, judgments, and decisions **based on beliefs.**

## The Subconscious Mind is...

The subconscious is the part of the mind responsible for all our involuntary actions like our heartbeat and breathing rate. It does not evaluate, make decisions, or pass judgment. It just is. It does not determine if something is "right" or "wrong."

The subconscious is much like the software of a computer. On the computer keyboard, if we press the key for the letter "a," we will see the letter "a" on the screen, even though we may have wanted to see "t." Just as a computer can only do what it has been programmed to do, we can only do as we are programmed to do.

©Tessa Cason, 2022.

Our programming is determined by our beliefs. Beliefs and memories are "stored" in the subconscious.

## Three Rules of the Subconscious Mind

Three rules of the subconscious mind include:

1. Personal. It only understands "I," "me," "myself." First-person.

2. Positive. The subconscious does not hear the word "no." When you say, "I am not going to eat that piece of cake," the subconscious mind hears, "Yummm! Cake! I am going to eat a piece of that cake!"

3. Present time. Time does not exist for the subconscious. The only time it knows is "now," present time. "I'm going to start my diet tomorrow." "Tomorrow" never comes; thus, the diet never starts.

> Beliefs precede all of our thoughts, feelings, decisions, choices, actions, reactions, and experiences...
>
> Our beliefs and memories are stored in the subconscious mind.
>
> If we want to make changes in our lives, we have to change the programming, the dysfunctional beliefs in the subconscious.
>
> Three rules of the Subconscious Mind:
> Personal
> Positive
> Present time

©Tessa Cason, 2022.

# Chapter 5
# How Does EFT Tapping Work?

1. Acceptance: The last part of the tapping statement, we say, "I totally and completely accept myself." **Acceptance brings us into present time.** We can only heal if we are in present time.

2. Addresses the current dysfunctional beliefs on a subconscious level: To make changes in our lives, we have to change the dysfunctional beliefs on a subconscious level. The middle part of the tapping statements are the "instructions" for the subconscious. **To make changes in our lives, we only care what the subconscious hears.**

3. Pattern interrupt: Dysfunctional memories and/or beliefs block energy from flowing freely along the meridians. Tapping is a pattern interrupt that disrupts the flow of energy to allow our **body's own Infinite Wisdom to come forth for healing.** (Tapping both sides does not act as a pattern interrupt.)

4. Mis-direct: One role of the physical body is to protect us. When our hand is too close to a flame, our body automatically pulls our hand back to safety. An EFT Tapping statement that agrees with the current belief is more effective. The physical body is less likely to sabotage the tapping if it agrees with the current belief.

For the EFT Taping statement "I fear change":

* This statement appeases the physical body since it agrees with the current belief.
* The tapping disrupts the energy flow so our Truth can come forth.

The body will always gravitate to health, wealth, and well-being when the conditions allow it. EFT Tapping weeds the garden so the blossoms can bloom more easily and effortlessly.

# Chapter 6
# Benefits of Using EFT Tapping

* The last part of the statement is, "I totally and completely **accept** myself." **Acceptance** brings us into present time. Healing can only take place when we are in present time.

* By tapping, we are **calling forth our Truths**. The keyword here is **"our."** Not anyone else's. If my name is "Lucas," tapping the statement "Even though my name is Troy," my name will not change to Troy.

* Tapping **calls forth our body's Infinite Wisdom.** When we cut our finger, our body knows how to heal the cut itself. Once the dysfunctional emotions, experiences, and beliefs have been "deleted," our body **automatically** gravitates to health, wealth, wisdom, peace, love, joy…

* By changing dysfunctional beliefs and emotions on a subconscious level, the changes we make with EFT are **permanent.**

* EFT Tapping can change:
    Beliefs
    Emotions
    Self-images
    Our story
    Thoughts
    Mind chatter
    Painful memories

* EFT Tapping can neutralize stored memories that block energy along the meridians.

* EFT Tapping can desensitize emotions. We might have a difficult person in our life who ignores us and/or criticizes us, so we tap the statement: "This difficult person [or their name] ignores and criticizes me."

Tapping does not mean they will no longer ignore and/or criticize us; however, it can **desensitize us,** so we are no longer affected by their behavior. Once we have desensitized the emotions, our perception and mental thinking improve. We are better able to make informed decisions. We don't take and make everything personal. Our health is not negatively impacted. Our heart doesn't beat 100 beats/minute. Smoke stops coming out of our ears, and our faces don't turn red with anger and frustration.

©Tessa Cason, 2021.

# Chapter 7
# What We Say As We Tap Is VERY Important!

All of our beliefs are programmed into our subconscious minds. If we want to change our lives, we have to delete the dysfunctional beliefs on a subconscious level. The statements we make as we tap are the instructions for the subconscious mind.

THE TAPPING STATEMENTS WE WAY AS WE ARE TAPPING ARE CRITICAL FOR THIS TO HAPPEN!

Example: You get in a taxi. Several hours later, you still have not arrived at your destination. "*Why?*" you ask. Because you did not give the destination to the taxi driver!

Tapping without saying an adequate tapping statement is like riding in a cab without giving the cab driver our destination!

For EFT Tapping to be MOST EFFECTIVE the Tapping Statement is CRITICAL!

EFT Tapping allows us to delete the dysfunctional beliefs on a subconscious level. The statements we make as we tap are instructions to the subconscious mind so our Truth can come forth.

©Tessa Cason, 2021.

# Chapter 8
# Using a Negative EFT Tapping Statement

Our beliefs **precede** all of our thoughts, feelings, decisions, choices, actions, reactions, and experiences.

If we want to make changes in our lives, we have to change the dysfunctional beliefs. Our beliefs are stored in the subconscious.

To change our lives, to change a belief, we only care what the subconscious hears when we tap. The subconscious does not hear the word "no." When we say, "I am not going to eat that piece of cake," the subconscious hears, "Yummm, cake!"

Example, if we don't believe we have what it takes to be successful and we tap the statement, "I have what it takes to be successful," the body could sabotage the tapping. We could tap and it won't clear.

Instead, if the statement we make is, "I do not have what it takes to be successful," the **"not"** appeases the physical body and the subconscious hears, "I have what it takes to be successful!"

©Tessa Cason, 2022.

# Chapter 9
# EFT Tapping Statements Are Most Effective When They Agree With Current Beliefs

The EFT Tapping statement is **more successful when** it **is something the body currently believes.**

> The body is less likely to sabotage an EFT Tapping statement that agrees with the current belief.

One role of the physical body is to protect us from harm. (For example, if our hand gets too close to a flame, our body will pull our hand back to safety.) The body is less likely to sabotage the statement and the process if the EFT Tapping statement agrees with the current belief. Thus, it appeases the physical body.

For example, if our desire is prosperity and wealth and we tap the statement, "I am prosperous now," the body could sabotage the tapping by forgetting what we were saying, getting easily distracted, or our mind chatter may remind us we are not prosperous. We could tap and the statement, most likely, will not clear.

If the statement we say is "I am not prosperous now," the "**not**" appeases the physical body, and the subconscious hears, "I am prosperous now!"

# Chapter 10
# The Very First EFT Tapping Statement to Tap

The very first EFT Tapping statement I have clients and students tap is, "It is not okay or safe for my life to change." I have muscle tested this statement with more than a thousand people. Not one person tested strong that it was okay or safe for their life to change. (Muscle testing is a way in which we can converse with the body, bypassing the conscious mind.)

> How effective can EFT or any therapy be if it is not okay or safe for our lives to change?

Since our lives are constantly changing, if it is not okay or safe for our lives to change, every time our lives change, it creates stress for the body. Stress creates another whole set of issues for ourselves, our lives, and our bodies.

# Chapter 11
# One Statement per Round of EFT vs Multiple Statements per Round of EFT

Laser-focused Tapping vs Round Robin Tapping

Same Statement for all the Tapping Points in One Round
vs Multiple Statements in One Round of Tapping (Scripts)

Two styles of tapping for different purposes. One style is best for healing dysfunctional beliefs. The other style is best for healing emotions, desensitizing a story, situation, and/or memory.

I found that the laser-focused, one statement for a round of tapping was most effective for healing the beliefs. Multiple statements per round of tapping is great at healing emotions, desensitizing a story, situation, and/or memory.

## SAME STATEMENT FOR ALL THE TAPPING POINTS IN ONE ROUND

After tapping the statement, "It's not okay for my life to change," and we are able to take a deep breath, we know the statement cleared. Then we tap, "I'm not ready for my life to change," and we are not able to take a deep breath, most likely, the statement did not clear.

Knowing the statement did not clear, we can focus on the reasons, excuses, and/or beliefs about not being ready to change our lives.

* Maybe the changes we need to make would require more of us than we want to give.
* Maybe we don't feel we have the abilities we would need if our life changed.
* Maybe we don't feel our support system, the people in our life, would support the changes we want to make.

Follow-up tapping statements for "I'm not ready for my life to change" could be:

* I do not have the abilities change would require.
* I am afraid of change.
* Others will not support the changes I want to make in my life.
* I am not able to make the changes I want to make.
* I do not have the courage that change would require.
* I am too old to change.

©Tessa Cason, 2022.

Tapping the same statement at all eight points is most effective for clearing beliefs. When a statement does not clear, we can focus on the reasons, excuses, and/or dysfunctional beliefs that blocked the statement from clearing.

## Multiple Statements in One Round of Tapping (Scripts/Round Robin)

Tapping multiple statements in one round, also known as Scripts or Round Robin tapping, is excellent for healing a story, and desensitizing a memory or story.

Healing a broken heart, to desensitize the heartache of the break up, the following script/statements could be said, one statement/point:

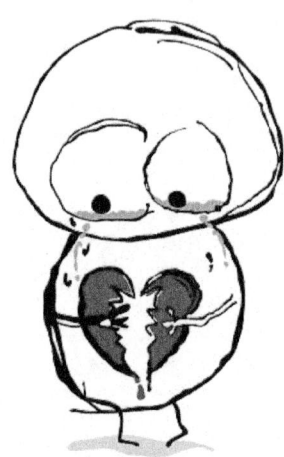

* My boyfriend broke up with me.
* I am heartbroken.
* He said he doesn't love me anymore.
* I do not know how I can go on without him.
* It hurts.
* I am sad he doesn't love me anymore.
* I am sad our relationship is over.
* I will never find anyone like him ever again.

### Reframing:

Reframing is a Neuro Linguistic Programming (NLP) term. It is a way to view and experience emotions, situations, and/or behaviors in a more positive manner.

At the end of round robin tapping, we can introduce statements to "reframe" the situation.

An example of reframing could be:

* I want this chocolate.
* Maybe eating chocolate is wanting to reconnect to my childhood.
* Maybe eating sugar is a way of being loved.
* Maybe I can find a different way of being loved.

Round robin tapping, scripts, can desensitize the hurt and pain. It can heal the pain of our story. It may not rewrite the beliefs. To clear out the beliefs, it would be necessary to look at the reasons the relationship didn't work and why our heart is broken, or why we crave chocolate.

Round robin/script tapping can also be done by just tapping the side of the hand.

©Tessa Cason, 2022.

### Side of Hand Tapping to Desensitize a Story, Situation, and/or Memory

Just as in the round robin tapping/scripts, we said different statements, one after the other, we can say the same statements and just tap the side of the hand.

If a memory still "haunts" us, embarrasses us, and/or affects our actions in any way, this technique might be perfect to neutralize the memory.

For example:

As Sasha remembers the first dance she attended as a teen-ager, tears well up in her eyes. She starts to tap the side of the hand (SOH) as she tells her story:

My best friend, Samantha and I, were so excited about attending our first high school dance. We weren't old enough to drive so Sam's dad dropped us off in front of the high school auditorium where the dance was held.

*(Continue to tap the SOH)* We were in awe of how the auditorium was transformed into a palace. Sofas were placed around a hardwood dance floor in the center of the room. We promised each other we would be there for the other throughout the night so neither of us would be stranded alone.

*(Continue to tap the SOH)* Well, along came Billy McDaniels. Sam had had a crush on Billy since third grade. He asked her to dance and I never saw her again for the rest of the night.

*(Continue to tap the SOH)* Those three hours were probably the worst night of my entire life! No one asked me to dance. Every time I joined a group of girls, a new song would begin, and every one of them was asked to dance, everyone except me. I don't know why no one asked me to dance. I felt ugly, abandoned, and undesirable! Talk about being a wallflower. I thought I was invisible. I wanted to hide from embarrassment.

*(Continue to tap the SOH)* This was back in the days before cell phones. The auditorium didn't have a payphone to call my parents to come and get me. I had to endure three hours of humiliation watching every single girl be asked to dance EXCEPT me.

*(Continue to tap the SOH)* I never attended another high school dance again!

Whether we tap the side of the hand or the eight tapping points, the result is the same. Round robin tapping can desensitize emotions and memories very effectively.

There are different styles of EFT Tapping.
Find the style that works best for your desired result.

©Tessa Cason, 2022.

# Chapter 12
# Walking Backwards EFT (Backing Up)

As I was working with a client, they had an issue that was not clearing. Knowing that movement helps to clear issues, I decided to have the person stand up and walk backward. Literally, walk backward, step after step, facing forward while their feet moved backward.

Surprise, surprise, it worked. Every statement cleared as she backed up.

The next client came in. I had him walk backwards, and it worked with clearing issues for him as well. Both clients were somewhat athletic and did workout. I wanted to know if the Backing Up would work with non-athletic people. I was teaching an EFT class the next day. At the end of the class, we all backed up together. And, IT WORKED!

Let's say we want to process, "I will never be comfortable in the world." Stand up. Make sure nothing is behind you. Then walk backward while facing forward and say, "I will never be comfortable in the world. I will never be comfortable in the world. I will never be comfortable in the world. I will never be comfortable in the world." Repeat the phrase six - eight times.

When we back up, we say the same statement we would have made if we were tapping. We don't have to say the "Even though" or the last remainder phrase, "I totally and completely accept myself."

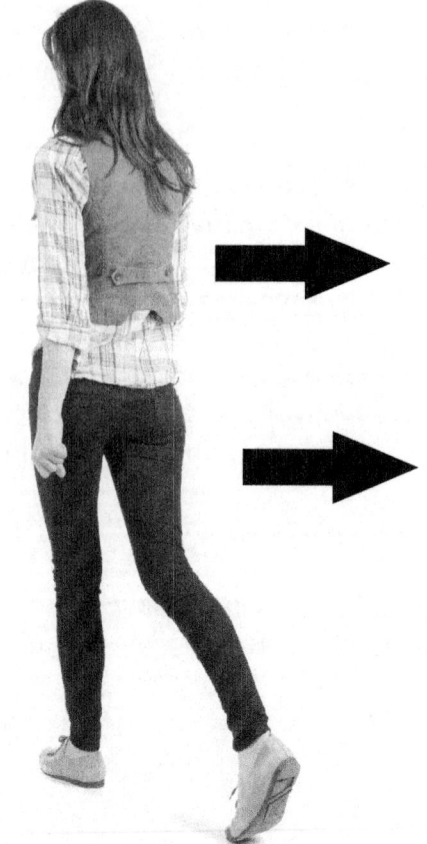

> Walking forward represents forward movement in our lives. Walking backward represents the past.
>
> Physical movement can help clear emotional issues and facilitate change.
>
> Walking backward undoes the past and helps to clear, heal, and transform an issue in our lives.

©Tessa Cason, 2022.

# Chapter 13
# Intensity Level

One measure of knowing how much an issue has been resolved is to begin, before tapping, by giving the issue an intensity number (IL) between 1 and 10, with 10 being high.

For example, we want a romantic partnership, yet we haven't met "the one." Thinking about a romantic relationship happening, what is the likelihood, on a scale of 1 - 10, with 10 being very likely and 1, not likely at all, of a romantic relationship happening?

Okay. We give ourselves a 2. Now, let's start tapping!

When asked what the issues might be, "Well," we say, "it does not seem as if the people who I want, want me."

Great tapping statement. Tap, "Even though the people I want don't want me, I totally and completely accept myself." After tapping, we check in with ourselves; the IL has gone up to a 4, so it is now a little bit more likely.

What comes to mind now? "No one will find me desirable." Great tapping statement. "Even though no one will find me desirable, I totally and completely accept myself." Check the IL. How likely? 5. Cool! Progress.

What comes to mind now? "I'm not comfortable being vulnerable in romantic relationships." Great tapping statement. "Even though I'm not comfortable being vulnerable in a romantic relationship, I totally and completely accept myself." Check the IL. Now it is a 6. Still progress.

What comes to mind now? "Well, it feels like if I am in a relationship, I will lose a lot of my freedom." Make this into a tapping statement. "Even though I will lose my freedom when I am in a relationship, I totally and completely accept myself." The IL has gone up to a 7.

What comes to mind now? "Oh, if I was in a relationship, I would have to be accountable to someone!" Make this into a tapping statement: "Even though, I would have to be accountable to someone if I was in a relationship, I totally and completely accept myself." Wow…the IL is 9, very likely!

Giving an issue an Intensity Level gives at the beginning and throughout the session gives us an indication of the progress we are making with resolving and/or healing that issue in our lives.

©Tessa Cason, 2022.

# Chapter 14
# Yawning and Taking a Deep Breath

From Traditional Chinese Medicine, we know that when chi (energy) flows freely through the meridians, the body is healthy and balanced. Physical, mental, and/or emotional illness can result when the energy is blocked.

Dysfunctional beliefs and emotions produce blocks along the meridians, blocking energy from flowing freely in the body.

With EFT Tapping, as we tap, we release the blocks. As blocked energy is able to flow more freely, the body can now "breathe a sigh of relief." Yawning is that sigh of relief.

If, after tapping, we can take a complete, deep, full, and satisfying breath, we know that an EFT Tapping statement has cleared. This yawn is an indication that an EFT Tapping statement has cleared.

If the yawn or breath is not a full, deep breath then the statement did not clear completely.

# Chapter 15
# Integration...What Happens After Tapping

After tapping, our system needs some downtime for integration to take place. When the physical body and the mind are "idle," integration can take place.

Sometimes, in the first 24 hours after tapping, we might find ourselves vegging more than normal, sleeping more than normal, or more tired than normal. This downtime is needed to integrate the new changes.

After installing a new program into our computer, sometimes we have to reboot the computer (shut down and restart) for the new program to be integrated into the system.

After tapping, our bodies need to reboot. We need some downtime. When we sleep, the new changes are integrated.

HEALING BEGINS NATURALLY AFTER THE BODY HAS HAD A CHANCE TO INTEGRATE.

Sometimes, after tapping, we forget the intensity of our pain and think that feeling better had nothing to do with tapping. Something so simple could not possibly create the improvement in our state of mind!

When we cut our finger, once it is healed, we don't even remember cutting our finger. As we move toward health, wealth, and well-being, sometimes we don't remember how unhappy, restless, or isolated we once felt.

# Chapter 16
# EFT Tapping Doesn't Work for Me

Why might EFT Tapping not be working?

* The tapping statement might not be worded such that a dysfunctional belief and/or emotion is addressed and eliminated.
* The style (laser-focused style vs round robin) of tapping may not be effective for the statement to be cleared.
* The EFT Tapping statement is only addressing a symptom and **not the cause of the issue**.

FOR EFT TAPPING TO BE EFFECTIVE, THE CAUSE OF THE ISSUE NEEDS TO BE HEALED.

* Having an awareness of our issues does not heal the dysfunctional beliefs.
* Forgiving ourselves and/or someone else does not heal the dysfunctional beliefs.
* Talk therapy does not heal the dysfunctional beliefs.
* Desensitizing the emotions does not heal the dysfunctional beliefs.
* Healing the experience of a hurtful event does not change the dysfunctional beliefs.

## EFT Tapping works best when

1) the statements are worded to eliminate the dysfunctional beliefs,
2) the most effective style of tapping is utilized, and
3) we are healing the cause, not just the symptoms.

©Tessa Cason, 2022.

# Chapter 17
# What to Do if an EFT Tapping Statement Does Not Clear

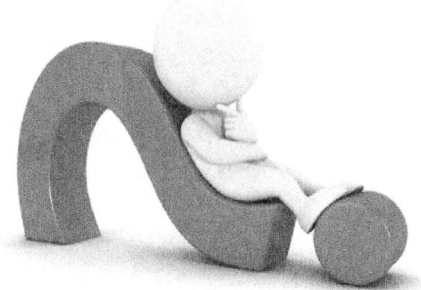

When a statement might not clear, turn the statement into a question. The statement, "It's not okay for me to be powerful," didn't clear. **Turn the tapping statement into a question:** "Why isn't it okay for me to be powerful?"

The answer might be:

* Powerful people are ruthless and heartless.
* I am afraid of being powerful.
* Being powerful would change me for the worse.
* Power corrupts.
* People would laugh at me if I tried being powerful.
* I would have to give up my fears and anxieties to be powerful.
* I might be called aggressive if I tried being powerful.
* I do not have the abilities, skills, or qualities to be powerful.
* Others would make fun of me if I tried being powerful.
* Powerful people are thoughtless and self-centered.

With these beliefs, it might not be okay or safe to be powerful or even explore the idea of being powerful. The statements above are tapping statements. Tap the answer to the question.

After tapping the answer to the question, revisit the original statement that did not clear. Most likely, it will now be cleared, and you will be able to take a full, deep, and complete breath.

# Chapter 18
# Science and EFT Tapping Research

EFT has been researched in more than ten countries by more than sixty investigators whose results have been published in more than twenty different peer-reviewed journals. Two leading researchers are Dawson Church, Ph.D. and David Feinstein, Ph.D.

Dr. Dawson Church, a leading expert on energy psychology and an EFT master, has gathered all the research information, and it can be found on this website: www.EFTUniverse.com.

## Two Research Studies

### 1) Harvard Medical School Studies and the Brain's Stress Response

Studies at the Harvard Medical School reveal that stimulating the body's meridian points significantly reduces activity in a part of the brain called the amygdala.

The amygdala can be thought of as the body's alarm system. When the body is experiencing trauma or fear, the amygdala is triggered, and the body is flooded with cortisol, also known as the stress hormone. The stress response sets up an intricate chain reaction.

The studies showed that stimulating or tapping points along the meridians such as EFT Tapping, drastically reduced and/or eliminated the stress response and the resulting chain reaction.

### 2) Dr. Dawson Church and Cortisol Reduction

Another significant study was conducted by Dr. Dawson Church. He studied the impact an hour's tapping session had on the cortisol levels of eighty-three subjects. He also measured the cortisol levels of people who received traditional talk therapy and those of a third group who received no treatment at all.

On average, for the eighty-three subjects who completed an hour tapping session, cortisol levels were reduced by 24%. Some subjects experienced a 50% reduction in cortisol levels.

The subjects who completed one hour of traditional talk therapy and those who had completed neither session did not experience any significant cortisol reduction.

# Chapter 19
# Is Lowering the Cortisol Level Enough to Permanently Change Our Lives?

Several things can lower our cortisol (stress hormone) levels including:
* Power posing
* Meditating
* Laughing
* Exercising regularly
* Listening to music
* Getting a massage
* Eliminating caffeine from our diet
* Eating a balanced, nutritious meal and eliminating processed food

Would performing any of the above activities lower our cortisol level enough to permanently change our lives? Only if the activity eliminates the dysfunctional beliefs on a subconscious level.

All of our thoughts, feelings, actions, reactions, choices, and decisions are preceded by a belief. To change our lives, the dysfunctional beliefs must be eliminated.

Power posing, listening to music, or eating a balanced meal will not permanently change our lives. Exercising will help our physical body but will not delete our dysfunctional beliefs. Laughing will bring us into the present so we will not be drawn into our fears or anger, but it will not change our lives. Meditating helps us to center and balance, but will not change our lives on a permanent basis.

To change our lives, we must be able to recognize, acknowledge, and take ownership of that which we want to change then delete the dysfunctional emotions and beliefs that preceded that what we want to change on a subconscious level.

EFT Tapping will delete dysfunctional emotions and beliefs on a subconscious level if we provide the correct "instructions" to our subconscious mind. We must word the tapping statements in the subconscious' language. We must word the tapping statement so the subconscious mind hears what we want to eliminate.

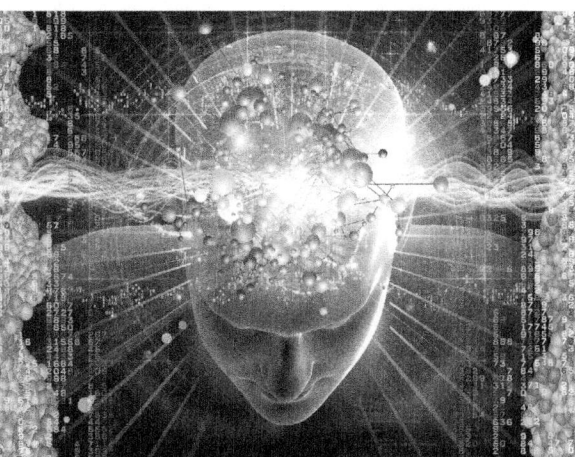

©Tessa Cason, 2022.

# Chapter 20
# Tapping Affirmations

* I am healthy and happy.
* Wealth is pouring into my life.
* I radiate love and happiness.
* I have the perfect job for me.
* I am successful in whatever I do.

If we were to tap "I am healthy and happy now" and we are not, most likely, as we are tapping, we might think, "Yeah, right. Sure. I am healthy and happy. My life sucks. I hate my job. I am always broke. There is never enough money…"

The body knows this is not true. We are not healthy and happy now. When we tap, we might have difficulty remembering what we are saying, lose focus and concentration, and/or the mind drifts.

*An EFT Tapping statement is most effective **when** it matches our current belief.*

The subconscious does not hear the word "No." One way of tapping affirmations and, at the same time, putting in the positives is to put the word "no" into the tapping statements.

* I am **not** healthy and happy. Subconscious hears: I am healthy and happy.
* Wealth is **not** pouring into my life. Subconscious hears: Wealth is pouring into my life.
* I **do not** radiate love and happiness. Subconscious hears: I radiate love and happiness.
* I **do not** have the perfect job for me. Subconscious hears: I have the perfect job for me.
* I am **not** successful in whatever I do. Subconscious hears: I am successful in whatever I do.

If we repeat affirmations over and over and over before we clear the affirmation with EFT Tapping, repeating the affirmation numerous times will have little effect except to create circumstances in our lives so we can be confronted with the beliefs that do not align with the affirmation.

©Tessa Cason, 2022.

# Chapter 21
## Finishing Touches – Positive Statements

Some like to finish their tapping with statements that are centering and calming. If this is you, then you might want to try the 16 statements on the next page or make up those that you like. The statements can be said in any order that works for you.

| Tapping Location | Statement |
| --- | --- |
| Eyebrow | All is well in my life. |
| Temple | Every day in every way |
| Under the Eye | I am fulfilled in every way, every day. |
| Under the Nose | My blessings appears in rich |
| Under the Lips | I am an excellent steward of wealth and am blessed with great abundance. |
| Under the Collarbone Knob | I take complete responsibility |
| Under the Arm | I have all the tools, skills, and |
| Top back part of the Head | I know I will be able to handle anything |
| Eyebrow | All my dreams, hopes, wishes, and goals |
| Temple | Divine love expressing through me, |
| Under the Eye | I am comfortable with my life changing. |
| Under the Nose | I am able to create all that I desire. |
| Under the Lips | I know what needs to be done and |
| Under the Collarbone Knob | My health is perfect in every way, physically, |
| Under the Arm | I invite into my subconscious Archangel Raphael to heal all that needs to be forgiven, released, and redeemed. Cleanse me and free me from it now. |
| Top back part of the Head | The light of God surrounds me. The love of God enfolds me. The power of God protects me. The presence of God watches over and flows through me. |

# Chapter 22
# How to Use This Book

1. The statements are divided into sections. Read through the statements in one section. As you read a statement, notice if you have any reaction to the statement or feel the statement might be true for you. If so, note the number for that statement.

2. Once you have completed reading all the statements in one section, go back and reread the statements you noted and rate them on a scale of 1 – 10, with 10 being a "biggie."

3. List the top statements.

4. From this list, select one and describe how it plays out in your life. It is important to recognize and identify the pattern. What are the consequences of having this belief? Is there a trigger? How does it begin? How does it benefit you? How has it harmed you? There will be a different example listed in each section.

5. Tap the statements. Statements can be combined for scripts...a different statement on each of the different tapping points in one round of tapping.

6. Describe any flashbacks or memories that you might have had as you were tapping out the statements. Describe any ah-has, insights, and/or thoughts you might have had as a result of tapping the statements.

7. After tapping all the statements, review them to determine if you still have a reaction to any of the statements. If you do, you have several options. One, put a "Why" before the statement. Tap out the answer. Secondly, note that this statement may not have cleared and continue on to the next section. Most likely, after additional statements are tapped, statements that may not have cleared, will clear without having to tap the statement again.

8. Allow some downtime for integration and for the body to heal.

9. The number of sections you do at a time will be up to you. Initially, you might want to do one section to determine if you get tired and need to have some downtime after tapping.

10. The day after tapping, again review the statements you tapped to determine if you still have a reaction. If you do, follow the instructions in #7.

©Tessa Cason, 2022.

# 1 – 20 EFT Tapping Statements

*Ships are safe in the harbor,
but that's not what ships are for.*

*William Shedd*

1. I am not safe.
2. My fears are real.
3. I freeze in a crisis.
4. I am a drama junkie.
5. Fear inhibits my life.
6. I am afraid of people.
7. Fear is not an illusion.
8. I am a people-pleaser.
9. I am full of self-doubt.
10. I am paralyzed by fear.
11. I am afraid of intimacy.
12. My fear keeps me safe.
13. I am weak, weak, weak.
14. It will never be my turn.
15. I am afraid of letting go.
16. I am afraid of the future.
17. I don't believe in myself.
18. I am an emotional wreck.
19. I am defective, a mistake.
20. Fear stops me every time.

# Journaling Pages for Statements 1 – 20

*It is essential to differentiate between healthy and unhealthy fear. The anxieties and worries that pervade our daily lives, the real troublemakers, are not born from healthy fear, but from neurotic fear. Healthy fear stands guard responsibly, informing us immediately of real danger. Neurotic fear works around the clock, exaggerating and even inventing potential dangers. Healthy fear is about protection and guidance. Neurotic fear is about the need to be in control. Healthy fear inspires us to do what can be done in the present. Neurotic fear speaks to us endlessly about everything that could possibly go wrong tomorrow, or the next day, or next year.*

*Thom Rutledge*


1. From the tapping statements between 1 – 20, list the top seven statements that you thought or felt applied to you:

1.

2.

3.

4.

5.

6.

7.


2. From this list of seven statements, select one and describe how it plays out in your life. Give an example or two. It is important to recognize and identify the pattern. Is there a trigger? How does it begin? How has it benefited you? How has it harmed you? For instance, does fear stop you every time? Is it fear that stops you or is it the lack of skill, talent, desire, and/or ability?


3. Tap out the top 7 statements.


4. As you were tapping out the statements, did you have any flashback or memories of the past, any additional insights, and/or ah-ha thoughts? If so, write them down. Make note of them.

©Tessa Cason, 2022.

# 21 – 40 EFT Tapping Statements

*Courage is not the absence of fear, rather the judgement
that something else is more important than fear.*

*Ambrose Redmoon*

21. I know I am a loser, a failure.
22. I allow fear to inhibit my life.
23. Fear is my excuse for failure.
24. I am intimidated by my fears.
25. I know I am stupid and dumb.
26. I am afraid of being powerful.
27. I will never be free of my fear.
28. I expect the worse to happen.
29. I'm the gloom and doom type.
30. I am afraid of my own shadow.
31. I do fear by avoiding intimacy.
32. Fear fuels my need to control.
33. The glass is always half empty.
34. Life is full of traps and threats.
35. I am anxious about everything.
36. I am afraid of making mistakes.
37. I will never make it on my own.
38. No one asks much of a coward.
39. The world is a hazardous place.
40. Fear is my constant companion.

# Journaling Pages for Statements 21 – 40

*The fear associated with venturing into the unknown is perfectly normal and to be expected. While it is normal to feel a certain amount of fear and apprehension when making changes, it is destructive to allow this fear to immobilize us, causing us to remain stuck in the status quo. We can instead use the fear and transform it into motivation to take positive action.*

*Jim Donovan*

1. From the tapping statements between 1 – 20, list the top seven statements that you thought or felt applied to you:

1.

2.

3.

4.

5.

6.

7.

2. From this list of seven statements, select one and describe how it plays out in your life. Give an example or two. It is important to recognize and identify the pattern. Is there a trigger? How does it begin? How has it benefited you? How has it harmed you? For instance, is fear your constant companion? What we focus on, expands. Do you focus on your fear, your failures, your losses, and thus get more of what you fear? Or do you focus on your joy, your successful, and your journey?

3. Tap out the top 7 statements.

4. As you were tapping out the statements, did you have any flashback or memories of the past, any additional insights, and/or ah-ha thoughts? If so, write them down. Make note of them.

©Tessa Cason, 2022.

# 41 – 60 EFT Tapping Statements

*There comes a time when the risk to remain tight in a bud will be more painful than the risk it takes to blossom.*

*Anais Nin*

41. Life is just too damn hard.
42. I am afraid of being alone.
43. I fear everyone's opinions.
44. I am afraid of growing old.
45. I cannot conquer my fears.
46. I am afraid to be by myself.
47. I am afraid of the unknown.
48. My fear will never go away.
49. Fear is in charge of my life.
50. I will fail again if I try again.
51. I am afraid of losing control.
52. The world is full of dangers.
53. I will never master my fears.
54. I do fear by isolating myself.
55. I numb out when I am afraid.
56. I am afraid of World War III.
57. I am less than everyone else.
58. I cannot get beyond my fear.
59. I am not in charge of my life.
60. My fears have control of me.

# Journaling Pages for Statements 41 - 60

*Many games are lost before a step is run. Many cowards fail before their work begins. Think big and your deeds will grow. Think small and you will fall behind. Think you can win, you will. It is all in the state of mind. The history of the world is full of men who rose to leadership, by sheer force of self-confidence, bravery, and tenacity.*

*Mahatma Gandhi*


1. From the tapping statements between 1 - 20, list the top seven statements that you thought or felt applied to you:

1.

2.

3.

4.

5.

6.

7.


2. From this list of seven statements, select one and describe how it plays out in your life. Give an example or two. It is important to recognize and identify the pattern. Is there a trigger? How does it begin? How has it benefited you? How has it harmed you? For instance, is the world full of danger? The world is also full of joy, happiness, love, and fulfillment. Which do you choose to see and experience?


3. Tap out the top 7 statements.


4. As you were tapping out the statements, did you have any flashback or memories of the past, any additional insights, and/or ah-ha thoughts? If so, write them down. Make note of them.

# 61 – 80 EFT Tapping Statements

*Never be afraid to try something new. Amateurs built the ark, professionals built the Titanic.*

*Unknown*

61. I shy away from social activities.
62. I will get hurt again if I try again.
63. I am not willing to face my fears.
64. I am afraid I will die before I live.
65. "Just do it," doesn't work for me.
66. Bottom line of my fears is failing.
67. Fear is my only protective shield.
68. I have an intense need for safety.
69. Fear is my excuse for everything.
70. I can't stop the negative self-talk.
71. I know I am worthless and foolish.
72. My thoughts focus mainly on fear.
73. My fears are real and not illusions.
74. I am reduced to tears by my fears.
75. I am not free to explore the world.
76. Bottom line of my fear is rejection.
77. My biggest fear is being homeless.
78. I am afraid to be my authentic self.
79. I don't see fear as a warning signal.
80. I know I am weak and incompetent.

# Journaling Pages for Statements 61 – 80

*Some parents plant seeds of fear, shame, or guilt. As we grow into adulthood, these seeds grow into invisible weeds that invade our lives in ways we never dreamt they could. Their tendrils do harm to our relationships, our careers, and our families. Adult children of toxic parents suffer from damaged self-confidence and self-esteem which leads to self-destructive behaviors. They feel worthless, unlovable, and inadequate. These patterns continue into our adulthood.*

*Susan Forward*

1. From the tapping statements between 1 – 20, list the top seven statements that you thought or felt applied to you:

1.

2.

3.

4.

5.

6.

7.

2. From this list of seven statements, select one and describe how it plays out in your life. Give an example or two. It is important to recognize and identify the pattern. Is there a trigger? How does it begin? How has it benefited you? How has it harmed you? For instance, do you believe you will be hurt again if you try again? Do you understand how you got hurt the first time? If not, it's understandable why you believe you will be hurt again. You have not learn and grown from the first experience and thus, it is most likely, you would be hurt again.

3. Tap out the top 7 statements.

4. As you were tapping out the statements, did you have any flashback or memories of the past, any additional insights, and/or ah-ha thoughts? If so, write them down. Make note of them.

©Tessa Cason, 2022.

# 81 – 100 EFT Tapping Statements

*It is easy to be brave from a safe distance.*

*Aesop*

81. I know I will make the wrong decision.
82. Releasing my fear will not set me free.
83. I don't know how to conquer my fears.
84. I am a prisoner of my own insecurities.
85. I never learned coping skills as a child.
86. I will never be able to do my life alone.
87. I am unable to get away from my fears.
88. Fear is a major stumbling block for me.
89. I am afraid of love, peace, and success.
90. Fear is the noose that is strangling me.
91. I am immobilized by my indecisiveness.
92. Being afraid prepares me for the worst.
93. I am afraid I cannot take care of myself.
94. I allow my fears to restrict my activities.
95. I am not competent enough to succeed.
96. I am obsessed with keeping myself safe.
97. I am not good enough and never will be.
98. My fear keeps me from being authentic.
99. I have a lot of doubt and indecisiveness.
100. I never developed confidence as a child.

# Journaling Pages for Statements 81 - 100

*Try a thing you haven't done three times. Once, to get over the fear of doing it.
Twice, to learn how to do it. And a third time to figure out whether you like it or not.*

*Virgil Thomson*

1. From the tapping statements between 1 - 20, list the top seven statements that you thought or felt applied to you:

1.

2.

3.

4.

5.

6.

7.

2. From this list of seven statements, select one and describe how it plays out in your life. Give an example or two. It is important to recognize and identify the pattern. Is there a trigger? How does it begin? How has it benefited you? How has it harmed you? For instance, does your fear keeps you from being authentic? Do you know who your authentic self is? If so, is your concern rejection and not being good enough? Would the issue then be fear or not being good enough? To change, we have to be able to recognize, acknowledge, and take ownership of what doesn't work in our lives.

3. Tap out the top 7 statements.

4. As you were tapping out the statements, did you have any flashback or memories of the past, any additional insights, and/or ah-ha thoughts? If so, write them down. Make note of them.

©Tessa Cason, 2022.

# 101 – 120 EFT Tapping Statements

*I have learned over the years that when one's mind is made up, this diminishes fear. Knowing what must be done does away with fear.*

*Rosa Parks*

101. I allow fear to limit my possibilities.
102. Life is frightening and intimidating.
103. I am afraid of ending up a bag lady.
104. I will not be able to give up my fear.
105. The world is not a safe place to live.
106. I feel ignored, invisible, and frazzled.
107. I check and recheck everything I do.
108. I do fear by being overly controlling.
109. I allow my fears to restrict all my fun.
110. I have a lot of uncertainty and worry.
111. I know I am inadequate and helpless.
112. The world is full of traps and threats.
113. My life is dull, routine, and mundane.
114. I feel resentful, powerless, and angry.
115. I have trouble speaking up for myself.
116. Life is a burden and not an adventure.
117. I have no idea who I am or what I feel.
118. Bottom line of my fears is succeeding.
119. I have trouble initiating conversations.
120. It is not okay/safe for me to be strong.

# Journaling Pages for Statements 101 - 120

*What is it about us human beings that makes us so willing to stay in an unhealthy situation just because it is familiar to us? Why would we rather remain in a dead-end job, continue in a destructive relationship, or stay "stuck" in a lifestyle we dislike simply because we are in a comfort zone of familiarity? Why is our attitude so often "I may be stuck in the mud, but at least it's my mud"? Is our fear of change so strong that we are willing to allow our lives to slip quietly by rather than face our fears and make changes to improve situations?*

*Jim Donovan*

1. From the tapping statements between 1 - 20, list the top seven statements that you thought or felt applied to you:

1.

2.

3.

4.

5.

6.

7.

2. From this list of seven statements, select one and describe how it plays out in your life. Give an example or two. It is important to recognize and identify the pattern. Is there a trigger? How does it begin? How has it benefited you? How has it harmed you? For instance, do you feel ignored? Do others not want to deal with your fears so they ignore you? There are a lot of advantages to being ignored. Less is asked of you or expected of you. Maybe you prefer not to be asked and your fears allow you to be ignored.

3. Tap out the top 7 statements.

4. As you were tapping out the statements, did you have any flashback or memories of the past, any additional insights, and/or ah-ha thoughts? If so, write them down. Make note of them.

©Tessa Cason, 2022.

# 121 – 140 EFT Tapping Statements

*Fear fuels our negative and judgmental thoughts and our need to control things. Fear underlies guilt and shame and anger. Every difficult emotion we experience represents some kind of threat – a threat to our self-esteem or to the stability of a relationship, even to our right to be alive. And threat translates to fear. Start with any difficult emotion you choose, get on the elevator, press B for Basement, and there, below guilt and shame and anger, below the negativity and the judgments, you will find it: fear. Fear hides inside seemingly less severe emotions such as anxiety, worry, and nervousness, each of which has various levels and shadings.*

Thom Rutledge

121. I wouldn't be so frightened if I was perfect.
122. I won't even begin because I will surely fail.
123. Bottom line of my fear is that I don't matter.
124. I am afraid of joy, sweetness, and happiness.
125. Bottom line of my fears is being abandoned.
126. I am easily alarmed over potential problems.
127. It is not okay/safe for me to give up my fear.
128. I remain in fear to justify focusing on myself.
129. My fear prohibits me from accepting myself.
130. I know I will never be beautiful or cherished.
131. I am afraid to communicate my true feelings.
132. I focus on my hardships, tragedies and crises.
133. I am not willing to accept the good in my life.
134. Fear is more powerful and forceful than I am.
135. I don't have the energy to rise above my fear.
136. There are lots advantages to being a coward.
137. So many things I get to avoid by being afraid.
138. I am choosing fear over peace and happiness.
139. I feel overwhelmed, defeated, and victimized.
140. I have no one to help me get through my fear.

©Tessa Cason, 2022.

# Journaling Pages for Statements 121 – 140

*Curiosity will conquer fear even more than bravery will.*

*James Stephens*

1. From the tapping statements between 1 – 20, list the top seven statements that you thought or felt applied to you:

1.

2.

3.

4.

5.

6.

7.

2. From this list of seven statements, select one and describe how it plays out in your life. Give an example or two. It is important to recognize and identify the pattern. Is there a trigger? How does it begin? How has it benefited you? How has it harmed you? For instance, do you feel defeated and overwhelmed? The game of life doesn't build character. It reveals it. If you feel defeated, what skills have you attempted to learn, what resources have you acquired, what strategies have you put in place to help you handle the stresses of life?

3. Tap out the top 7 statements.

4. As you were tapping out the statements, did you have any flashback or memories of the past, any additional insights, and/or ah-ha thoughts? If so, write them down. Make note of them.

# 141 – 160 EFT Tapping Statements

*Don't be afraid to go out on a limb.*
*That's where the fruit is.*

*H. Jackson Browne*

141. Being fearful takes away all my options.
142. Bottom line of my fear is not belonging.
143. I will be disappointed again if I try again.
144. I am afraid of feeling and looking foolish.
145. My life is stagnant as a result of my fears.
146. I live in the future instead of the present.
147. Fear is standing in the way of my destiny.
148. I will not take one ounce of risk in my life.
149. I try to live up to unrealistic expectations.
150. My fear keeps me from feeling truly alive.
151. My fears keep me from fulfilling my goals.
152. I am afraid of what others might do to me.
153. I need protection from the big, bad world.
154. My fears keep me awake night after night.
155. I allow my fears to restrict my excitement.
156. My heart starts to race when I feel fearful.
157. The older I get, the more fearful I become.
158. Bottom line of my fears is not being loved.
159. It is not okay/safe for me to feel fully alive.
160. I have difficulty getting a good night's rest.

# Journaling Pages for Statements 141 - 160

*Once men are caught up in an event, they cease
to be afraid. Only the unknown frightens men.*

*Antoine de Saint Exupéry*


1. From the tapping statements between 1 - 20, list the top seven statements that you thought or felt applied to you:

1.

2.

3.

4.

5.

6.

7.


2. From this list of seven statements, select one and describe how it plays out in your life. Give an example or two. It is important to recognize and identify the pattern. Is there a trigger? How does it begin? How has it benefited you? How has it harmed you? For instance, does fear keeping you from fulfilling your goals? Is it really fear that is keeping you from fulfilling your goals or could it be you have not developed the skills necessary to succeed? Is it easier to blame the fear rather than to develop new skills and abilities?


3. Tap out the top 7 statements.


4. As you were tapping out the statements, did you have any flashback or memories of the past, any additional insights, and/or ah-ha thoughts? If so, write them down. Make note of them.

# 161 – 180 EFT Tapping Statements

*I learned that courage was not the absence of fear, but the triumph over it.
The brave man is not he who does not feel afraid, but he who conquers that fear.*

*Nelson Mandela*

161. My vocabulary is full of "can't," "buts," "if only."
162. I know my fears are irrational, but I'm still afraid.
163. I don't have the confidence to live my life boldly.
164. Bottom line of my fears is being financially broke.
165. I feel uncomfortable when others compliment me.
166. I retreat and withdraw when I am afraid of people.
167. I am not capable of releasing the fear I feel within.
168. I hyperventilate when I am facing something I fear.
169. I will hide until I have the courage to face my fears.
170. My fear robs me of being empowered and focused.
171. I'm not capable of protecting myself and/or others.
172. I am not willing to confront and overcome my fears.
173. I don't want to own my power, strength, or courage.
174. I avoid situations instead of acknowledging my fear.
175. I am not willing to relax and let life flow through me.
176. I don't know the answers that I'm supposed to know.
177. I accommodate my fears rather than deal with them.
178. Bottom line of my fears is never being good enough.
179. My fear prevents me from going places I want to go.
180. It is much easier to be a coward than to be successful.

©Tessa Cason, 2022.

# Journaling Pages for Statements 161 – 180

*Inaction breeds doubt and fear. Action breeds confidence and courage. If you want to conquer fear, do not sit home and think about it. Go out and get busy.*

*Dale Carnegie*

1. From the tapping statements between 1 – 20, list the top seven statements that you thought or felt applied to you:

1.

2.

3.

4.

5.

6.

7.

2. From this list of seven statements, select one and describe how it plays out in your life. Give an example or two. It is important to recognize and identify the pattern. Is there a trigger? How does it begin? How has it benefited you? How has it harmed you? For instance, is it easier to be a coward than to be successful? Do you have the desires, talents, abilities, and experiences needed to be successful? Or is it easier to slide into fear?

3. Tap out the top 7 statements.

4. As you were tapping out the statements, did you have any flashback or memories of the past, any additional insights, and/or ah-ha thoughts? If so, write them down. Make note of them.

# 181 – 200 EFT Tapping Statements

*Never let the fear of striking out get in your way.*
*Babe Ruth*

181. I don't have to be powerful when I am in fear.
182. I am afraid there will never be enough for me.
183. I get angry instead of acknowledging my fear.
184. I get drunk instead of acknowledging my fear.
185. Bottom line of my fears is being alone forever.
186. I know I will never be courageous or powerful.
187. I avoid feeling so I don't have to face my fears.
188. It is safer being a coward than being powerful.
189. Fear keeps me from moving forward in my life.
190. I am not powerful enough to dissolve my fears.
191. I'm not willing to make mistakes or look foolish.
192. I never have a moment of peace, relief, or calm.
193. Bottom line of my fears is disappointing others.
194. I am hesitant to venture out of my comfort zone.
195. The world is a threatening and frightening place.
196. I need someone stronger than me to protect me.
197. Fear fuels my negative and judgmental thoughts.
198. Bottom line of my fears is never being cherished.
199. I am always exhausted and emotionally depleted.
200. My parents were extremely overprotective of me.

# Journaling Pages for Statements 181 – 200

*Fear has its use, but cowardice has none.*
*Mahatma Gandhi*

1. From the tapping statements between 1 – 20, list the top seven statements that you thought or felt applied to you:

1.

2.

3.

4.

5.

6.

7.

2. From this list of seven statements, select one and describe how it plays out in your life. Give an example or two. It is important to recognize and identify the pattern. Is there a trigger? How does it begin? How has it benefited you? How has it harmed you? For instance, are you willing to make mistakes? Are you willing to learn? The way in which we learn is through trial and error. If you are not willing to learn, is this because you don't think you can learn?

3. Tap out the top 7 statements.

4. As you were tapping out the statements, did you have any flashback or memories of the past, any additional insights, and/or ah-ha thoughts? If so, write them down. Make note of them.

# 201 – 220 EFT Tapping Statements

*The enemy is fear. We think it is hate; but, it is fear.*

*Gandhi*

201. I'm waiting for someone to rescue me from my fears.
202. My fear prohibits me from realizing my full potential.
203. My fear is the only thing keeping me from being hurt.
204. I don't have the tools and skills to overcome my fears.
205. I am waiting for permission to live my life with passion.
206. I am afraid of being rejected, unloved, and abandoned.
207. I am afraid of _____, _____ and _____.
208. No one will ask anything of me because I am a coward.
209. I can't handle _____, _____, and _____.
210. I fear high floors of a building and flying in an airplane.
211. I withdraw from others and give up when I feel inferior.
212. My fear robs me of my power, passion, and confidence.
213. My fear robs me of being centered and in present time.
214. I don't know how to break out of the prison of my fears.
215. My fear robs me of my integrity, peace of mind, and joy.
216. I will deal with my fears when I feel better about myself.
217. My fear prevents me from doing the things I want to do.
218. I exhaust myself worrying about every possible problem.
219. I avoid situations that might cause me stress and anxiety.
220. I don't trust my ability to handle whatever comes my way.

# Journaling Pages for Statements 201 - 220

*The very things we now wish that we could hold onto and keep safe from change were themselves originally produced by changes. And many of those changes, in their day, looked just as daunting as any in the present do. No matter how solid and comfortable and necessary the status quo feels today, it was once new, untried and uncomfortable. Change is not only the path ahead, but it is also the path behind us, the one which we traveled along to wherever we are now trying to stay.*

*William Bridges*

1. From the tapping statements between 1 - 20, list the top seven statements that you thought or felt applied to you:

1.

2.

3.

4.

5.

6.

7.

2. From this list of seven statements, select one and describe how it plays out in your life. Give an example or two. It is important to recognize and identify the pattern. Is there a trigger? How does it begin? How has it benefited you? How has it harmed you? For instance, does your fear prevents you from doing the things you want? Is it fear that stops you or could it be your lack of confidence, desire, or talents?

3. Tap out the top 7 statements.

4. As you were tapping out the statements, did you have any flashback or memories of the past, any additional insights, and/or ah-ha thoughts? If so, write them down. Make note of them.

©Tessa Cason, 2022.

# 221 – 240 EFT Tapping Statements

*Fear: False Evidence Appearing Real.*
*Unknown*

221. My fear keeps me from making the most of every moment.
222. My fear keeps me from being accountable and responsible.
223. My fears are the excuse I use so I can hide and be invisible.
224. My fear is disproportionate to the nature of the uncertainty.
225. I am still fearful even after the source of the fear has ended.
226. My fears are the excuse I use so I don't have to be powerful.
227. I would rather be afraid than move outside my comfort zone.
228. I don't have the energy to raise above and conquer my fears.
229. My fear is the only thing keeping me from getting hurt again.
230. It is easier to be fearful than to focus on what I want to create.
231. I don't have the determination to face and overcome my fears.
232. I never learned how to handle challenging situations as a child.
233. I want a guarantee that if I take a risk, nothing bad will happen.
234. I don't know how to handle disappointment, resentment, or failure.
235. I push people out of my life that want me to move beyond my fear.
236. I am waiting for the right circumstances to begin living my life fully.
237. It is not okay/safe for me to fully feel, experience, and express love.
238. I come up to a brick wall every time I want to move beyond my fears.
239. I put up a front of being strong so others won't know the coward I am.
240. My fears are the excuse I use so I don't have to move forward in my life.

# Journaling Pages for Statements 221 – 240

*Fear is only as deep as the mind allows.*

*Japanese Proverb*

1. From the tapping statements between 1 – 20, list the top seven statements that you thought or felt applied to you:

1.

2.

3.

4.

5.

6.

7.

2. From this list of seven statements, select one and describe how it plays out in your life. Give an example or two. It is important to recognize and identify the pattern. Is there a trigger? How does it begin? How has it benefited you? How has it harmed you? For instance, did your parents handle all your challenging situations when you were young and now you don't know how to handle complex and challenging circumstances in your life? If so, what can you do to start developing your self-confidence? What baby step can you begin with?

3. Tap out the top 7 statements.

4. As you were tapping out the statements, did you have any flashback or memories of the past, any additional insights, and/or ah-ha thoughts? If so, write them down. Make note of them.

# Books by Tessa Cason

## All Things EFT Tapping Manual

* Why does EFT Tapping work for some and not for others?
* How do you personalize EFT Tapping to be most effective for you?
* What is the very first tapping statement you need to tap?

This manual provides instructions on how to heal our disappointments, regrets, and painful memories.

EFT Tapping information has instructions on what to do if a tapping statement does not clear, what to do if tapping doesn't work for you, and how to write your own tapping statements.

We must eliminate the dysfunctional beliefs if we want to make changes in our lives. EFT Tapping can do just that. EFT Tapping is a simple, yet very powerful tool to heal our beliefs, emotions, painful memories, and stories.

## 500 EFT Tapping Statements for Moving Out of Survival

Survival is stress on steroids. It's feeling anxious and not good enough. Survival may be the most important topic we can heal within ourselves. Survival is programmed into our DNA.

Ella returned home from the market with her three year old daughter to find a note from her husband that he did not want to be married any longer. Under the note were divorce papers, the number of the divorce attorney, and $500.

Wanting to be able to give her daughter a wonderful childhood, she had to figure out how to survive and thrive. This is her story and the tapping statements she tapped.

Dr. John Montgomery says, "All 'negative,' or distressing, emotions, like fear, disgust, or anxiety, can be thought of as 'survival-mode' emotions: they signal that our survival and well-being may be at risk."

## 80 EFT Tapping Statements for Change

If it is not okay or safe for our lives to change, every time our lives change, the body is subjected to a tremendous amount of stress.

After graduating from high school, Charlie's dad told Charlie he could continue to live at home, but he would be charged room and board. At 18, Charlie was now financially responsible for himself. He was able to find a job and moved out.

Within a year, circumstances forced Charlie to move back home. Day after day, Charlie rode the bus to work. After work, he rode the bus home. One day as Charlie was riding the bus to work, he noticed another regular rider, Dan, tapping his head.

Together Dan and Charlie began tapping. Find out the results of their tapping and the statements they tapped.

## 300 EFT Tapping Statements for Self-defeating Behaviors, Victim, Self-pity

Tom had lots of excuses and reasons for his lack of "results." His boss, Robert MacGregor, saw the potential Tom had and asked his longtime friend, Sam Anderson, a life coach, to work with Tom. Read Tom's story to understand how Tom was able to step into his potential.

Self defeating behaviors take us away from our goals, from what we want, leaving us feeling exhausted, disempowered, and defeated. Self defeating thoughts are the negative thoughts we have about ourselves and/or the world around us such as "I'm not good enough", "I have to be perfect to be accepted."

Most likely, you have tried to change the self-defeating and self sabotage behavior, yet here you are with the same patterns.

## 100 EFT Tapping Statements for Feeling Fulfilled

John wasn't sure what would fulfill him. He loved his job and didn't want to find a new career, but he wasn't feeling fulfilled in his life. With the help of his wife, John found what would be fulfilling.

Fulfillment is a simple formula, actually. It's the follow-through that might be the problem.

What would prevent you from being fulfilled? Do you know what the blocks might be, the reason you remain out of sync, unfulfilled? Is it about leaving your comfort zone or maybe it's that you allow your limitations to define your life?

It is possible to remove the blocks, heal the beliefs on the subconscious level, and move toward your desire for fulfillment. To do so, we need a powerful tool. One such tool is EFT Tapping, the Emotional Freedom Technique.

## 100 EFT Tapping Statements for Being Extraordinary!

Accomplishing extraordinary performances, having incredible successes, or earning large sums of money does not equate to an extraordinary person. This book is about discovering your extraordinary character.

Extraordinary – Exceeding ordinary, beyond ordinary.

Extraordinary starts with the self, our character, depth, and strength of our being. It's being congruent, walking our talk. It is the love, compassion, and tenderness we show ourselves. It's the pure and highest essence of our being.

Rebecca was approaching a time in her life in which she was doing some soul searching and examining her life. She didn't feel extraordinary. In her late 50s, she felt she was just ordinary. She reached out to Tessa. The email exchanges are included in this book along with tapping statements.

## 400 EFT Tapping Statements for Being Empowered and Successful

Being empowered is not about brute strength or the height of our successes. It is the strength, substance, and character of our inner being. It is knowing that whatever life throws at us, we will prevail.

Ava has just started a business with her two very successful sisters. She wants the business with her sisters to succeed, yet, she doesn't feel empowered. She doesn't want to feel as if the business would fail because of her and is ready to do the emotional work so she matches her sisters' power and success.

Sophie, Ava's roommate and an EFT practitioner-in-training, works with Ava. With Sophie's help, Ava begins to feel empowered and that her business with her sisters will be a success.

## 300 EFT Tapping Statements for Healing the Self

We live in a complex world with multiple influences. At birth, it starts with our parents and soon afterwards, the influence of other family members (grandparents, siblings, etc.), TV shows, cartoon characters, commercials, and peers. As we get older, we have the influences of teachers, coaches, tutors, television and movie stars, pop stars, sports heroes, and so many other.

When Pete was offered a promotion at work and was not excited about something he had worked so hard to accomplish, he knew he needed to find some answers. He thought he was living his mother's version of his life. He didn't know what brought him joy.

With the help of EFT and an EFT Practitioner, Pete was able to discover his version of his life, what brought him joy, and how to live a fulfilling life.

## EFT Tapping for Anxiety, Fear, Anger, Self Pity, Courage (1,000 Tapping Statements)

Anxiety is a combination of 4 things: Unidentified Anger, Hurt, Fear, and Self Pity. We expect error, rejection, humiliation, and actually start to anticipate it.

When we are not in present time, we are either in the past or the future. Anger is the past. Fear is the future. Fear could actually be anger that we failed in the past and most likely will fail again in the future.

It takes courage on our part to heal the anxiety, identify the hurt, and to give up the self-pity. To heal, to thrive, and flourish, we need to address not only the Anxiety, but also the fear, anger, self pity, and hurt.

Healing is not about managing symptoms. It's about alleviating the cause of the symptoms.

## 80 EFT Tapping Statements for Feeling Less Than and Anxiety

Rene was excited for the year long mentoring program she enrolled in. *How wonderful*, she thought, *to be surrounded with like-minded people.* Five months into the program, she abruptly dropped out. Find out how her feeling Less Than and her Anxiety sabotaged her personal growth.

Anxiety has four parts: unidentified anger, hurt, fear, and self-pity. Living in a state of fear, we want a guarantee that our decisions and choices will produce the results or outcomes that we want. Feeling less than is played out in a cycle of shame, hopelessness, and self-pity. We feel shame about who we are, that we have little value, and that we are not good enough.

Feeling "less than" spirals down into depression, survival, and self-sabotage.

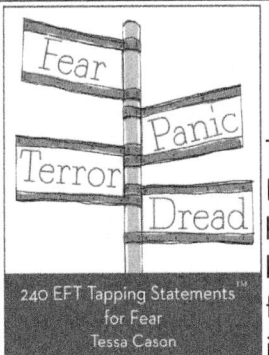

## 240 EFT Tapping Statements for Fear

Two months before school ended, Lennie was downsized from as a high school music teacher. When he was unable to find another job, fear crept into his thoughts. What if he couldn't find a job in music again? He wasn't qualified to do anything different. He was scared that he would not be able to support his family and they would end up homeless. He could feel the fear as his stomach was in knots.

Fear is that sense of dread, knots in the stomach, chill that runs down our spine, and the inability to breathe. We all know it. Fight-Flight-Freeze.

Fear is a self-protection mechanism. It is an internal alarm system that alerts us to potential harm. When we are in present time, we have the courage, awareness, wisdom, discernment, and confidence to identify and handle that which could cause us harm.

## 80 EFT Tapping Statements for Anxiety and Worry

"I just can't do this anymore," said Frank to his wife Mary. "You worry about everything. When we got married, your anxiety was something you did every now and then. But now you are paranoid about everything. I leave for work and you act like you are never going to see me again."

Anxiety is a combination of 4 things: unidentified anger, hurt, fear, self-pity. We expect error, rejection, humiliation, and actually start to anticipate it. It is an internal response to a perceived threat to our well-being. We feel threatened by an abstract, unknown danger that could harm us in the future.

Worry is a mild form of anxiety. Worry is a tendency to mull over and over and over anxiety-provoking thoughts. Worry is thinking, in an obsessive way, about something that has happened or will happen. Going over something again and again and asking, "What will I do? What should I have done?"

## 200 EFT Tapping Statements for Healing a Broken Heart

She found someone who made her feel cherished, valued, and loved. Tall, dark, and handsome as well as aware, present and understanding. Matt was an awesome guy. He thought she, too, was someone special, intriguing, and awesome.

Matt was promoted at work which meant months away from home and thus, decided to end their relationship. Her best friend introduced her to EFT Tapping to heal her broken heart.

Time does not heal all. Healing the grief of a broken heart is not easy. Grief is more than sadness. Grief is a loss. Something of value is gone. Grief is an intense loss that breaks our hearts.

Over time, unhealed grief becomes anger, blame, resentment, and/or remorse. To heal a broken heart, we need to identify, acknowledge, and healed the dysfunctional beliefs. EFT Tapping can help.

## 400 EFT Tapping Statements for Dealing with Emotions

Did you see the movie Pleasantville with Tobey Maguire and Reese Witherspoon, two siblings who are trapped in a 1950s black and white TV show, set in a small midwest town where everything is seemingly perfect. David and Jennifer (Tobey and Reese) must pretend they are Bud and Mary Sue Parker, the son and daughter in the TV show.

Slowly, the town begins changing from black and white to color as the townspeople begin to experience emotions. Experiencing emotions is like adding color to a black and white movie. Color adds a depth, enjoyment, and pleasure to the movie. Emotions add depth, enjoyment, and pleasure to our lives.

Emotions add animation, richness, and warmth to our lives. They give our lives meaning and fullness. Without emotions, our lives would be as boring as watching a black and white movie.

## 80 EFT Tapping Statements for Abandonment

Feelings of abandonment can be triggered by the ending of a relationship as well as the death of an individual. Even though we may have an intellectual understanding of death, there is still a feeling of abandonment when someone we treasure dies. For a small child, they do not understand death. They may still expect the parent to return at any time.

Even though Kevin drove an expensive sports car he wasn't the playboy type. He wanted to settle down and start a family. Kevin felt Susan could be "the one." He wanted to talk to her about taking their relationship to the next level.

Before Kevin could talk to Susan, she ended the relationship because of his insecurities in their relationship. She felt it had to do with the abandonment of his mom when he was a child. This book gives you the exact statements that Kevin tapped to deal with his insecurities in relationships.

## EFT Tapping Statements for A Broken Heart: Abandonment, Anger, Depression, Grief, Emotional Healing (1,000 Statements)

Time does not heal all. When our hearts have been shattered, we feel nothing will ever be the same again. We are flooded with emotions... anger, grief, depression...

Regardless of what led to the broken heart, maybe a death, divorce, or a breakup, the result is the same...a broken heart. To heal a broken heart is not only about healing the grief, but also the feelings of abandonment, anger, and depression.

Being abandoned is a verb. It is something that "happens to us." The result of being abandoned is anger, grief, and depression. Grief is the sadness we experience when we have lost something of value.

In order to heal, we need to resolve the anger, grief, abandonment, and depression that resulted from our hearts being fractured.

## 200 ET Tapping Statements for Wealth

After graduating from high school, Amy looked for a job for a solid year unsuccessfully! She lacked the necessary experience and education. She felt like she was in a vicious cycle, going round and round and round. Finally, she was hired at a large chain store. For the last eight years, she has been shuffled, unhappily, between different departments.

As a birthday gift, her mom gave her a session with an EFT Practitioner to determine what she wanted to do with her life. Follow along with Amy on her journey to self-discovery.

What we manifest in our lives is a direct result of our beliefs. If we have a mentality of wealth and abundance, we will prosper and thrive.

Our beliefs determine the level of our wealth and abundance. To heal our dysfunctional beliefs, we need a powerful tool. EFT Tapping is one such tool.

## EFT Tapping Statements for Prosperity, Survival, Courage, Personal Power, Success
(1,000 Statements)

What we believe determines our prosperity. Our beliefs determine our thoughts and feelings which in turn determine our choices and decisions. Therefore, what we manifest in our lives is a direct result of our beliefs. If we are happy and joyful, we will see happiness in everything. If we are fearful, we will see fear around every corner. If we have a mentality of abundance, we will prosper.

It is difficult to be prosperous when we are stuck in survival. In survival, we feel disempowered to thrive. We can only survive. It takes Courage to step into our Personal Power and to Succeed. We need a powerful tool to heal our dysfunctional beliefs. EFT Tapping is one such tool.

In this book, there are 200 tapping statements for each of these 5 topics - Prosperity, Survival, Courage, Personal Power, and Success.

## 80 EFT Tapping Statements for Abundance, Wealth, Money

Abby just had her 46th birthday. She tried to celebrate but she didn't have anything to be happy about. Her parents had died in a car accident the Christmas before while driving home from her new home after celebrating Christmas. Both of her parents were real estate agents. She was their transaction coordinator. The three of them had their own offices, handling any real estate transaction that someone might need. Without them, she had no real estate transactions to coordinate.

Abby funds were running dry. She had applied for jobs without success. Abby talked to every one she and her parents knew in hopes of finding a job. With the slow real estate market, she was unable to find any work.

Find out how Abby turned her life around and the exact statements that Abby tapped to deal with her monetary issues.

## 400 EFT Tapping Statements for Dreams to Reality

Have you done everything you were supposed to do for your dreams to become reality? You were clear on what they were. You made your vision boards with lots of pictures of what you desired. You visualized them coming true and living that life. You've stated your affirmations over and over and over for their fulfillment. You released and allowed the Universe to handle the details. And, now, dust is collecting on your vision boards and you are still waiting for the Universe to handle the details.

Our dreams are our hopes and desires of what we want to come true one day. They are snapshots of what we want our future to be. Yet, sometimes, maybe most of the time, our dreams do not become reality and never manifest themselves in our lives. We gave up on our dreams a long time ago.

Jane shares her story of how she used EFT Tapping to turn her dreams into reality.

## 300 EFT Tapping Statements for Intuition

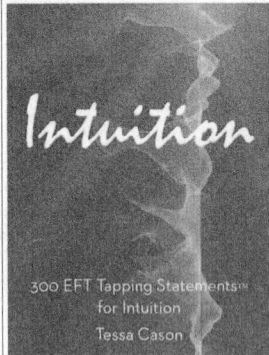

Quinn was one of Tessa's students in her Developing Your Intuition class. She had been hesitant to develop her intuition. One of her basic needs was Belonging. If she was intuitive, she might not belong and thus, realized this was part of her hesitation.

She also had a tendency to avoid which also wasn't conductive to developing her intuition. Tessa wrote out some EFT Tapping statements for her to tap:
* I ignore my inner voice.
* No one I know uses intuition.
* I'm too logical to be intuitive.
* Being intuitive is too complicated.

Included in this book are exercises and helpful hints to develop your intuition as well info on Symbolism, Colors, Number, Charkas, Asking Questions of Our Intuition, Archetypes, and 36 Possible Reasons We Took Physical Form.

## Emotional Significance of Human Body Parts.Chasing the Pain

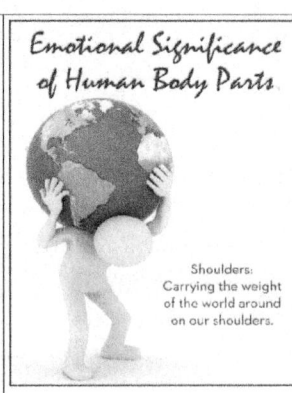

"We carry the weight of the world around on our shoulders." The emotional significance of the shoulder is about responsibility.

The body "talks" to us...in its language. To understand what the body is saying, we need to learn the body's language.

Jona greeted me at the airport gate on crutches. After hugging each other, she asked what the left ankle meant. I told her the left side of the body had to do with what's going on in the inside and the ankles had to do with commitments.

She had been dating a man for the last two months and he just proposed.

Chasing the Pain is a technique with EFT Tapping that as we tap for a physical pain we are experiencing, the original pain might disappear only to be felt in a different part of the body.

## 100 EFT Tapping Statements for Accepting Our Uniqueness and Being Different

Brian was an intelligent high school student with average grades. He tested high on all the assessment tests. Brian didn't think of himself as intelligent since his grades were only average. He didn't plan on going to college because he thought he wasn't smart enough and would flunk out.

His counselor knew otherwise and suggested Brian retake the tests to see if the tests were wrong. Find out Brian's scores after he retook the tests and how Mr. Cole introduced EFT Tapping to Brian.

If you were your unique self, do you fear being alone, rejected, or labeled as "undesirable?" Or maybe it's being laughed at and ridiculed for being different and unique?

When we play our lives safe, we end up feeling angry, anxious, powerless, hopeless, and depressed.

## Muscle Testing.Obstacles and Helpful Hints

Muscle testing is a method in which we can converse with the subconscious mind as well as the body's nervous system and energy field.

This book details 10 obstacles and 10 helpful hints to successfully muscle test.

One obstacle is that it is a necessity that the tester be someone that calibrates the same, or above, that of the testee, on David Hawkins' Map of Consciousness or be in the higher altitudes, 250 or higher, on the Map.

Helpful hint: When muscle testing, the tester and testee should not make eye contact with each other. With eye contact, the answer would be "our" energy instead of the "testee's" energy.

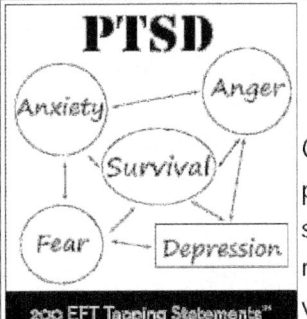
## 200 EFT Tapping Statements for PTSD

George believed that if he prepared for his death, it was signaling the Universe he was ready to die. George did die without preparing his wife.

George took care of everything. The only thing Helen had to take care of George.

After George died, she had no idea if they owned the home they lived in, if George had life insurance, how to pay bills, if they had money, if they did, where was it? She didn't know if George had left a will. She was not prepared for George's death or how to take care of everything that George took care of.

With the help of friends and EFT Tapping, Helen was able to heal and learn how to take care of everything that George once did.

Healing is not about managing symptoms. It is about alleviating the cause of the symptoms.

## EFT Tapping Statements for PTSD, Survival, Disempowered, Fear, Anger (1,200 Statements)

The potential exists for anyone that is in any life threatening situation in which they fear for their life, that believes death is imminent, to experience PTSD.

With PTSD, our Survival is at stake. As a result of our survival being threatened, we feel Disempowered to thrive. We can only survive. When we are caught in Survival, Fear is a prevalent emotion. When we feel Disempowered, Anger is just beneath the surface.

To heal, to thrive, and flourish, we need to address not only the PTSD, but also Survival and Feeling Disempowered, Fear, and Anger. (Thus, the 5 topics in this PTSD Workbook.)

Healing PTSD is a process in which we must desensitize, decrease, and heal the survival response. EFT Tapping is the best method to do so.

## 200 EFT Tapping Statements for Conflict

"Hi, Julia. So glad you called." Excitedly, I said, "I just finished decorating the house and I'm ready for Christmas!"

Not at all thrilled to be talking to her sister-on-law, Julia said, "That's why I'm calling. You don't mind if I host the family Christmas get-together, do you?"

A little surprised, I said, "Well, I do.

"Tough," she said. "I'm hosting Christmas this year."

This wasn't the first "conflict" with her sister-in-law. But, Audrey was a conflict coward and did not engage.

After EFT Tapping, Audrey overcame her issues with conflict. Find out how and who hosted Christmas that year!

## 80 EFT Tapping Statements for Anger

Doug was immensely proud of his son, Andy, until he watched his son (a high school senior) jeopardize his chance at an athletic scholarship to attend college. The count was 3-2, three balls and two strikes. The final pitch was thrown and Andy let it go by. The umpire shouts, "Strike!" Andy has just struck out.

"What's wrong with your eyes old man?" Andy shouts at the umpire. "That was a ball. It wasn't in the strike zone. Need instant replay so you can see it in slow motion? I'm not out!"

Andy, was following his father's example of being a rageaholic. EFT Tapping helped both Doug and Andy to take control of his life and his anger.

Anger is not right or wrong, healthy or unhealthy. It is the expression of anger that makes it right or wrong, healthy or unhealthy.

## 400 EFT Tapping Statements for Being a Champion

Jack was a professional runner that injured himself at the US Championships. He was unable to compete at the World Championship. The previous year, Jack had won gold at the World Championships. After six months, he still was not able to run even though the doctors assured him he should be able to run. He had exhausted all medical and physical therapy treatments without success or hope of being able to run pain-free.

Our of frustration, Jack decided to look at the mental piece with a transformation coach. Follow Jack's recovery back to the track through EFT Tapping.

Champions are rare. If being a champion was easy then everyone would be a champion and a champion would not be anything special. It is in the difficulty of the task that, once accomplished, makes a champion great.

## EFT Tapping Statements for Champion, Personal Power, Success, Self Confidence, Role Model (1,000 Statements)

Being a champion is more than just being successful. It is the achievement of excellence. It is more than just being competent. It is about stepping into one's power. It is more than just setting goals. It is the achievement of those goals with perseverance, dedication, and determination. It is not just about the practicing, training, and learning. It is the application and implementation of the training and learning into a competition and into everyday situations.

Champions are successful, but not all successful people are champions. Champions are powerful, but not all powerful people are champions. Champions are confident but not all confident people are champions. Champions dream big but not all people that dream big are champions.

## 300 EFT Tapping Statements for Dealing with Obnoxious People

Three siblings were each dealing with an obnoxious person in their lives. Katherine was dealing with a co-worker that took credit for her accomplishments.

Megan, a professional athlete, was distracted by a narcissistic team member that disrupted practice and thus, her performances at meets.

Peter was a very successful college student that had a Teaching Assistant jealous of everything that Peter was and the TA was not.

Read how each resolved and solved their issue with an obnoxious person.

## 80 EFT Tapping Statements for Self Esteem

Ron had driven a semi-trailer truck for 30 years for the same company. To celebrate his 60th birthday and 30 years of service, his company had a celebration for him. After the celebration, Ron's boss suggested that he find a job that was more age appropriate. Ron's lack of self-esteem was interfering with moving on with his life. This book gives you the exact statements that Ron tapped to heal his lack of self esteem, self respect, and self-pride.

From birth to about the age of seven, we learn self love from mom. From about the age of seven through twelve, from dad we learn self esteem, earned loved. Self esteem is about the feelings, respect, and pride we have in ourselves.

The lack of self esteem shows up in our lives as a lack self respect and/or pride in ourselves. This "lack" will taint every area of our lives.

## 340 EFT Tapping Statements for Healing From the Loss of a Loved One

Grief is more than sadness. It is more than unhappiness. Grief is a loss. Something of value is gone. Grief is an intense loss that breaks our heart. Loss can be the death of a loved one, a pet, a way of life, a job, a marriage, one's own imminent death. Grief is real.

Over time, unhealed grief becomes anger, resentment, blame, and/or remorse. We become someone that we are not. It takes courage to move through the grief and all the emotions buried deep within.

John's father died of a heart attack while gardening. A year after his death, John still was not able to move on or be happy. His wife handed him a business card of an EFT Practitioner and recommended therapy to heal the grief. After working with the Practitioner, John was able to find his joy again.

## 100 EFT Tapping Statements for Feeling Deserving

Sarah, a sophomore in college, was unsure of what to declare as her major. She met with a guidance counselor who wanted to chat first.

Sarah thought of herself as an accident since she had two older siblings who had already moved out of the house when she was five. Her parents had been looking forward to an empty nest, instead, they had a third child that was just starting school.

Sarah had felt undeserving her whole life, even though her parents loved her dearly and never treated her life an accident.

Travel the path Sarah walked with the counselor to finally feel deserving.

## 200 EFT Tapping Statements for Procrastination. What I Want to Do and What I Have to Do

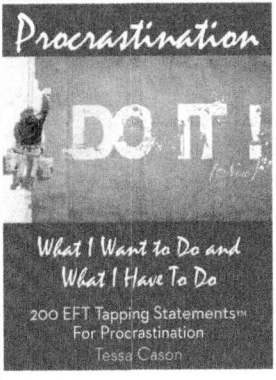

Procrastination is about avoiding.
* What are we avoiding?
* What are we afraid to find out?
* What are we not wanting to do?
* What are we not willing to face?

Is it:
* We don't have the tools and skills to do something.
* Rebellion
* Lack of motivation.
* Not knowing what needs to be done.
* Poor time management.

The list is long why we procrastinate and what it could be about. What do we do to heal our procrastination tendencies? EFT Tapping. To heal we have to be able to recognize, acknowledge, and take ownership of that which we want to heal. Then we have to delete the dysfunctional beliefs on the subconscious level. EFT is one such tool that can do just that.

## 80 EFT Tapping Statements for Relationship with Self

Stephanie, now 55 years old, used to be excited about life and about her life. That was 35 years ago. She was engaged to the love of her life. A month before the wedding her fiancée ran off with a beauty queen.

After 35 years, Stephanie still felt defeated, beaten, defective, broken, and flawed. She was still resentful. She had become comfortable in apathy because she did not know how to move beyond her self-pity.

With the help of EFT Tapping, Stephanie was able to heal her wounded self and begin to live life again.

Do you feel disconnected from yourself? Do you feel as if you could never be whole? Do you feel defeated by life? To change our lives, we have to be able to recognize, acknowledge, and take ownership of that which we want to change. Then heal the dysfunctional beliefs on a subconscious level. EFT Tapping can help.

## 700 EFT Tapping Statements for Weight, Emotional Eating, & Food Cravings

Emma's sister's wedding was fast approaching. She would be asked at the wedding how her diet was going.

Emma has struggled with her weight for the last 35 years, since high school. Out of desperation, Hannah began working with an EFT Practitioner. Follow her journey to healing the cause of her weight issues.

Excess weight, food cravings, emotional eating, and overeating are symptoms of deeper unresolved issues beneath the weight. Attempting to solve the problem by only dealing with the symptoms is ineffective and does not heal the issue.

Weight is the symptom. The usual programs for weight loss aren't working because they are attempting to solve the problem by dealing with the symptom instead of healing the cause.

## EFT Tapping Statements for Weight + Food Cravings, Anger, Grief, Not Good Enough, Failure (1,150 Statements)

Excess weight, food cravings, emotional eating, and overeating are symptoms of deeper issues beneath the weight. Attempting to solve the problem by only dealing with the symptoms is ineffective and does not heal the issue.

The usual programs for weight loss aren't working because they are attempting to solve the problem by dealing with the symptom instead of healing the cause.

IF WE WANT TO HEAL OUR WEIGHT ISSUES, WE NEED TO HEAL THE CAUSE...THE DYSFUNCTIONAL BELIEFS AND EMOTIONS.

HEALING IS NOT ABOUT MANAGING SYMPTOMS. IT'S ABOUT ALLEVIATING THE CAUSE OF THE SYMPTOMS.

## 80 EFT Tapping Statements for Addictions

Derrick's mom died when he was a senior in high school. His dad (an alcoholic) told Derrick that as soon as he graduated from high school, he was on his own.

The day that Derrick graduated from high school, he went down and enlisted in the army. In the army, he started to drink. A month after his enlistment concluded, he met a wonderful woman. They married and had a child.

One day when Derrick returned home from the bar, he found an empty house and a note. The note told him that since has unwilling to admit he was an alcoholic or to go to counseling, she was left with only one choice. That choice was to relocate herself and their daughter to some place safe, away from him.

Derrick felt he had nothing to live for. He discovered someone at work that was a recovering alcoholic. She introduced her secret, EFT Tapping, to Derrick.

## 80 EFT Tapping Statements for Weight and Emotional Eating

Excess weight is a symptom, not the cause of overeating and emotional eating.

The day that Tracy was graduating from UCLA, she received a phone call that her father had fallen and had been hospitalized. She was on the next flight home to Dallas. It was decided that her father needed surgery and that Tracy should stay on for a short while to care for her dad. No one asked Tracy what she wanted. But, she stayed anyway.

Seven months later, even though her father had mended, Tracy had become her father's caregiver. This is not what Tracy had planned to do with her life after graduating from college. Every month, over the course of the seven unhappy months, Tracy's weight spiraled up, until she was at her highest weight EVER.

This book gives you the exact statements that Tracy tapped to heal the cause of her weight gain.

# 80 EFT Tapping Statements for Manifesting a Romantic Relationship

Tanya tells the story about her best friend, Nica. Nica wants a relationship. She wants to be in love, the happily-ever-after kind of love. Nica is self-absorbed, self-centered, smart, and pretty.

Nica has had several long-term relationships but, never allows anyone close enough to get to know her. When she is in between boyfriends, she always whines:

* No man will ever want me.
* The odds are slim to none that I will find anyone.
* I have a bad track record with men so I give up.
* There will never be anyone for me.
* My desires will never be fulfilled.

Tanya is a tapper and finally Nica agrees to do some tapping as a last resort! The Tapping Statements that Nica tapped to manifest a relationship are listed in this eBook.

# 80 EFT Tapping Statements for Social Anxiety

In social settings, Johnny felt very awkward. He did not enjoy the limelight or any attention focused on him at all!

"Dude," Johnny's buddies would say. "When are you going to get over this fear of talking to a woman?" Johnny would laugh off their comments.

Social Anxiety – Dreading, fearing, and/or expecting to be rejected and/or humiliated by others in social settings.

* A feeling of discomfort, fear, dread, or worry that is centered on our interactions with other people.
* Fear of being judged negatively by others.
* Fear of being evaluated negatively by others.

Is there hope for those that have social anxiety? Yes. EFT Tapping. Tap the statements that Johnny tapped to overcome his social anxiety.

# 80 EFT Tapping Statements for Adult Children of Alcoholics

Did you have a parent that was an alcoholic? Do you have difficulty relating and connecting to others? Do you have a strong need to be perfect? Is your self-esteem low and judge yourself harshly? Do you have a fear of abandonment and rejection? If so, then EFT Tapping might help.

Rebecca had lost her 4th job. She was defensive, argumentative, and resentful. Rebecca knew her boss was right in firing her.

Rebecca's childhood was anything but idyllic. Her father was a raging alcoholic. She was terrified of his anger. Rebecca tried to be perfect so her dad couldn't find fault with her. Home life was hell. She had to grow up really fast and was never allow to be a kid or to play.

Rebecca did see an EFT Practitioner and was able to heal the anger, the need to be perfect, and other issues one has when they have an alcoholic parent.

# 200 EFT Tapping Statements for Knowing God

So many questions surround this topic, God. Does God exist or is God a fabrication? Is God for real or just a concept? If God does exist, then what is God's role in our lives?

Do our prayers get answered or are we praying in vain? Does God make mistakes? God created Lucifer and then kicked out a third of his angels from heaven along with Lucifer. Was Lucifer a mistake and all the angels that choose to follow Lucifer? Do we just want to believe that a supreme being really cares about us, gave us our lives' purpose, a mission, and a destiny? God is as varied as there are people.

Many have said that God gave humans the power of choice and free will. If this is true, the consequences of our actions are ours alone. Yet, there are those who believe that God could intervene. God should take action to protect and provide for us.

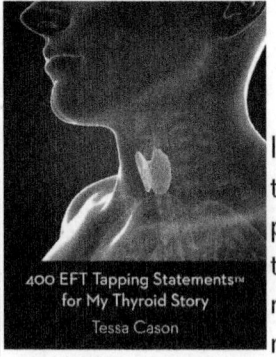

## 400 EFT Tapping Statements for My Thyroid Story

In 2005, I was diagnosed with thyroid cancer. I researched the potential cause and discovered that 20 years after exposure to natural gas, thyroid issues will result. 20 years previous to the diagnosis, I lived in a townhouse for 850 days that had a gas leak.

While pursuing healing modalities after the exposure to natural gas, I began to realize that about 50% of our health issues are emotionally produced. The other 50% are the result of environmental factors such as smoking, chemicals, accidents, and/or hereditary.

I did not believe my emotional issues caused the thyroid cancer. It was the result of an environmental factor outside myself. BUT, since the thyroid was affected, if I worked on the emotional issues that had to do with the thyroid, it should impact the thyroid cancer. That was my theory.

## 100 EFT Tapping Statements for Fear of Computers

Can you image strapping on your Jet pack to get to work? Traveling on the Hyperloop that travels at speeds up to 600 mph to visit a friend that lives in another state? Stepping into your self-driving car that chauffeurs you to the restaurant? Soon all of these will be a part of our lives.

Modern technology! Most everyone knows that the computer can answer most any question. Most every job today and jobs of the future require at least some knowledge of computers.

Grandmere was intimidated by the computer. Her motivation was her granddaughter would was moving to another country. Granddaughter wants her to learn to use the computer so they can Skype when she is out of the country. Read how Grandmere was able to overcome her anxiety and fear of the computer.

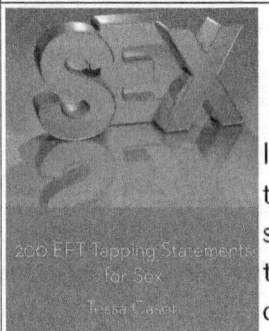

## 200 EFT Tapping Statements for Sex

Is sex about the act or is sex about the intimacy shared by the act? Is sex about the orgasms or is it about the connection, touching, and cuddling?

In most culture, sex/lovemaking/intercourse is not discussed, explored, or a polite topic of conversation. For a fulfilling and satisfying sexual relationship, communication is important, yet many couples find it difficult to talk about sex.

Can you talk to your partner about sex?
Are you comfortable with your sexuality?
Do you know your partner's sexual strategy?

Our attitude, beliefs, and emotions determine our thoughts and feeling about sex. Dysfunctional beliefs can interfere with a healthy, fulfilling, satisfying sexual relationship. If we want to make changes in our lives, we have to recognize, acknowledge, and take ownership of our dysfunctional beliefs and emotions.

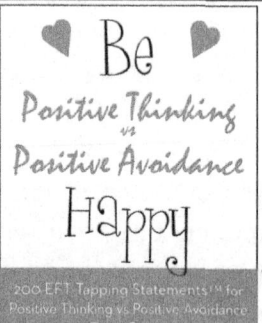

## 200 EFT Tapping Statements for Positive Thinking vs Positive Avoidance

If we keep piling more Band-Aids over a wound, the wound is still there. At some point, the wound needs to be examined, cleaned, and treated in order for heal.

Sometimes it is just "easier" to think positive when we really don't want to look at an issue. Positive Avoidance is denying the truth of a situation. It is a denial of our experience and our feelings about the situation.

When we try to push down our negative emotions, it is like trying to push a ball underwater. The ball pops back up.

Positive Thinking is the act of thinking good or affirmative thoughts, finding the silver lining around a dark cloud, and looking on the more favorable side of an event or condition. It is not denial, avoidance, or false optimism.

# Books and Kindles eBooks by Tessa Cason

80 EFT Tapping Statements for:
Abandonment
Abundance, Wealth, Money
Addictions
Adult Children of Alcoholics
Anger and Frustration
Anxiety and Worry
Change
"Less Than" and Anxiety
Manifesting a Romantic Relationship
Relationship with Self
Self Esteem
Social Anxiety
Weight and Emotional Eating

100 EFT Tapping Statements for Accepting Our Uniqueness and Being Different
100 EFT Tapping Statements for Being Extraordinary!
100 EFT Tapping Statements for Fear of Computers
100 EFT Tapping Statements for Feeling Deserving
100 EFT Tapping Statements for Feeling Fulfilled
200 EFT Tapping Statements for Conflict
200 EFT Tapping Statements for Healing a Broken Heart
200 EFT Tapping Statements for Knowing God
200 EFT Tapping Statements for Positive Thinking vs Positive Avoidance
200 EFT Tapping Statements for Procrastination
200 EFT Tapping Statements for PTSD
200 EFT Tapping Statements for Sex
200 EFT Tapping Statements for Wealth
240 EFT Tapping Statements for Fear
300 EFT Tapping Statements for Healing the Self
300 EFT Tapping Statements for Dealing with Obnoxious People
300 EFT Tapping Statements for Intuition
300 EFT Tapping Statements for Self-defeating Behaviors, Victim, Self-pity
340 EFT Tapping Statements for Healing From the Loss of a Loved One
400 EFT Tapping Statements for Being a Champion
400 EFT Tapping Statements for Being Empowered and Successful
400 EFT Tapping Statements for Dealing with Emotions
400 EFT Tapping Statements for Dreams to Reality
400 EFT Tapping Statements for My Thyroid Story

500 EFT Tapping Statements for Moving Out of Survival
700 EFT Tapping Statements for Weight, Emotional Eating, and Food Cravings
All Things EFT Tapping Manual
Emotional Significance of Human Body Parts
Muscle Testing – Obstacles and Helpful Hints

EFT TAPPING STATEMENTS FOR:
**A Broken Heart,** Abandonment, Anger, Depression, Grief, Emotional Healing
**Anxiety,** Fear, Anger, Self Pity, Change
**Champion,** Success, Personal Power, Self Confidence, Leader/Role Model
**Prosperity,** Survival, Courage, Personal Power, Success
**PTSD,** Disempowered, Survival, Fear, Anger
**Weight & Food Cravings,** Anger, Grief, Not Good Enough, Failure

OTHER BOOKS
Why we Crave What We Crave: The Archetypes of Food Cravings
How to Heal Our Food Cravings

EFT WORKBOOK AND JOURNAL FOR EVERYONE:
Abandonment
Abundance, Money, Prosperity
Addictions
Adult Children of Alcoholics
Anger, Apathy, Guilt
Anxiety/Worry
Being A Man
Being, Doing, Belonging
Champion
Change
Conflict
Courage
Dark Forces
Decision Making
Depression
Difficult/Toxic Parents
Difficult/Toxic People
Emotional Healing

Fear
Forgiveness
God
Grief
Happiness/Joy
Intuition
Leadership
Live Your Dreams
Life Purpose/Mission
People Pleaser
Perfectionism
Personal Power
Relationship w/Others
Relationship w/Self & Commitment to Self
Self Confidence
Self Worth/Esteem
Sex
Shame
Stress
Success
Survival
Transitions
Trust/Discernment
Victim, Self-pity, Self-Defeating Behavior, Shadow Self
Weight and Emotional Eating

Printed in Great Britain
by Amazon